Light
in the
Valley:

Herbert Vander Lugt

A CHRISTIAN VIEW
OF DEATH AND DYING

VICTOR BOOKS

a division of SP Publications, Inc., Wheaton, Illinois
Offices also in Fullerton, California • Whitby, Ontario, Canada • London, England

Scripture quotations are from the Scofield Reference
Bible, © 1967 by the Delegates of the Oxford Univer-
sity Press, Inc., New York. Used by permission.

Library of Congress Catalog Card Number: 77-3134
ISBN: 0-88207-504-7

© 1976, Radio Bible Class, Grand Rapids,
Michigan. VICTOR ADULT SHORT STUDY edition
published 1977. Used by permission.

VICTOR BOOKS
A division of SP Publications, Inc.,
P.O. Box 1825 • Wheaton, Illinois 60187

CONTENTS

PREFACE

The great resurrection chapter in the Bible closes with a thrilling rhapsody of Christian triumph: "O death, where is thy sting? O grave, where is thy victory? The sting of death is sin; and the strength of sin is the law. But thanks be to God, who giveth us the victory through our Lord Jesus Christ. Therefore, my beloved brethren, be ye steadfast, unmovable, always abounding in the work of the Lord, forasmuch as ye know that your labor is not in vain in the Lord" (1 Corinthians 15:55-58).

In these glowing words Paul personifies death as a defeated foe and hurls out this double challenge: "Where is your sting? Where is your victory?" Without waiting for a reply, he answers both questions, declaring that Jesus Christ removed death's sting by paying the price for sin, and defeated it by rising from the grave. Now, through faith in Christ, we are victors over death. Praise God!

The Christian view of death gives purpose to the present and fills the future with hope. It throws light upon our daily path and illuminates the shadowed valley that lies ahead. Believers should not be afraid to die. They should not live in dread of the passing of loved ones. They don't have to go to pieces when death invades their homes, nor be at a loss for words if called upon to comfort another in his time of grief.

The purpose of this book is to help you translate into everyday life the biblical teaching about death. God's children can demonstrate to the world that faith in Christ makes a tremendous difference in the way a person meets death and copes with the grief that accompanies it.

I want to thank David Egner, assistant to Richard De Haan, president of Radio Bible Class, for his careful editorial work. A word of appreciation is also due to Clair Hess, director of Radio Bible Class publications, for his assistance, and to Lois Weber for typing the manuscript.

Herbert Vander Lugt

1

What is Death?

Everybody occasionally thinks about dying. Death is a disturbing and mysterious reality no one can successfully avoid. I can't remember a time when I wasn't aware of it. As a little boy on a farm in North Dakota, I sometimes saw a wild animal dead in the field. I knew that when the proper market time came, our hogs, calves, and chickens would be slaughtered. Even though I didn't like to see any creature die, I soon accepted the idea that the life cycle which begins with birth inevitably ends with death.

Being inquisitive, I wondered what death really is, and what helped me more than anything else was the biblical teaching I received in my home and at church. I learned that when animals die, they simply go out of existence, but that a person lives on in another realm. When I was 7, my maternal grandfather, who had been living with us, succumbed to a heart condition. I well recall the funeral service, and I remember, as I watched the box being lowered into the earth, that I had absolute confidence that Grandpa was in Heaven with God.

Today, after spending many years in Christian work, I still believe what I learned about death in early boyhood. I have found that the teaching of the Bible meets every human need. It has delivered me from a morbid fear of dying. It has given me comfort and strength in my own times of bereavement. As a pastor, I have seen the eyes of people who were on the very brink of eternity sparkle with hope when I read the Scriptures to them. I've seen them smile when I reminded them of their security in Jesus Christ. And I have seen the faces of sorrowing people begin to brighten as I gave them the enlightening and comforting truths of the Gospel.

A few years ago a young girl who had been a neighbor of my parents was near death in a hospital in Grand Rapids. I didn't know the family well, but I was burdened for them and went to see them. When I walked into the room, I sensed immediately that the girl would die very soon. Her parents greeted me warmly and told me that she had given a clear testimony of having accepted Christ and was ready to meet the Savior. I prayed with them, and we talked about the promises of the Scriptures. Finally, the labored breathing stopped. The mother said quietly, "She's at rest. She's with the Lord." We thanked God together for the assurance He had given. The family remained calm and composed. How different this was from my experiences with people who had no faith in Jesus Christ! Christians really do face death differently. When you believe what the Bible says, you don't end up in a dark, foreboding canyon of hopelessness. The Scriptures give *light in the valley!*

I make no apologies for relying upon the Bible for answers to the questions related to death and dying. Its message brings dramatic results in those who believe it because it is the inspired Word of God and is accompanied by the ministry of the Holy Spirit. It focuses upon the death and resurrection of Jesus Christ, two well-attested historical events. It deals sympathetically yet realistically with man's deepest needs. It's the only logical place to go for information about the subject, the only authentic source of light for that "dark and lonesome valley" which everyone must walk someday.

In this book, therefore, I will present to you as clearly as I can the biblical teaching about death. I will answer from God's Word the questions about death and dying I was most often asked as a pastor by people facing this experience. If you are bereaved, my prayer is that your heart will be ministered to by these scriptural truths. If you are not sorrowing now, I trust the increased understanding of death you will receive from reading these pages will help you prepare for the time you must face it as a reality in your own life, either personally or through the loss of a loved one.

The first basic question I wish to answer is, "What is death?" Idealists have called it "an illusion," and romanticists speak of it as "man's last great venture." Poets have referred to it as "crossing the river" or "putting out to sea." Atheists say that it is the end of existence. But all such concepts are empty and offer no hope. The Bible presents four great truths which define death for us, and we will examine them in detail in this chapter. They are: (1) Physical death is separation of the soul from the body. (2) Spiritual death is separation from God. (3) Physical death is an enemy. (4) Physical death can be a friend.

Physical Death is Separation

The Bible teaches that physical death is the separation of the soul from the body. It is *not* the end of existence. Both the Old and the New Testaments consistently speak of it as a departure, in which the soul leaves the body and goes somewhere else. The vast majority of Christians are convinced that the soul of the one who believes in Jesus goes immediately to Heaven, where it enjoys the presence of Christ and awaits the day of resurrection. (Some disagree, and we will discuss the matter of the state between death and resurrection more thoroughly in a later chapter.) Yes, the Bible teaches that physical death is *not* termination, but a departure from one sphere of existence to enter another that is just as real.

The Old Testament speaks of the souls of the dead as going to a place called "sheol." In Genesis 25:8 we read, "Then Abraham died in a good old age, an old man, and full of years; and was gathered to his people." The writers of the Old Testament often used the phrase "gathered to his people" as a description of death. They believed that those who died went to a place of reunion with others who had preceded them. For example, when Jacob heard that his son Joseph had been killed, he said, "I will go down into sheol *unto my son* mourning" (Genesis 37:35). The patriarch thought Joseph had been devoured by a wild beast, yet he was convinced that he would see his son again. Jacob couldn't have been thinking that they would be buried in the same sepulcher, for he had absolutely no hope of finding the body. Therefore he must have expected that when he died, his soul would be reunited with that of

Joseph in sheol. So, while an exact and comprehensive definition of "sheol" may not be easy to formulate, no one can escape the clear teaching that the men of the Old Testament believed that at death they would leave their bodies and be reunited with their ancestors.

The New Testament is even more clear in defining physical death as separation of body and soul. Weary of the struggles of this world, the apostle Paul longed "to depart and to be with Christ, which is far better" (Philippians 1:23). He also wrote of his willingness "to be absent from the body, and to be present with the Lord" (2 Corinthians 5:8). Yes, he saw death as a departure," a leaving the body to be "present with the Lord."

In summary, physical death is defined in the Bible as the separation of the soul from the body. In the world of animals, this rift brings about the extinction of being. It appears that animals have some kind of soul, for the Hebrew term translated "living creature" in Genesis 1:21, 24 literally means "soul of life," and animals too have an immaterial aspect, though nothing in the Bible indicates that the animal possesses immortality. Man is unique, in that he was made in the image and likeness of God. The Bible tells us that when God created Adam, He "breathed into his nostrils the breath of life" (Genesis 2:7). Man's soul is therefore different from that of the animal. It does *not* go out of existence when it leaves the body, but lives forever. When we die, our souls leave our bodies and go immediately to be with Christ.

When physical death is defined in this way, even children can understand it. If a child is confronted with the death of an animal, we can take the opportunity to point out that the life has left the body, and that nothing remains but the carcass.

We can explain that birds and beasts don't think about God and don't have any concept of right and wrong or eternity. They have no longing for fellowship with the Lord, and no thought of continued existence after death. I have sometimes told youngsters that the prolific writer C. S. Lewis said he thought the Lord might bring back to life the animals that were the special pets of people here. But I hasten to add that I can find no Bible verses that prove this statement. I then explain that it's different with human beings. If a Christian has died, I assure the relatives that the body which is left behind is an empty shell in which their loved one no longer lives. Then I make it clear that the soul is in Heaven with the Lord Jesus.

Spiritual Death is Separation from God

A second basic biblical truth about death has to do with the state of the soul after it leaves the body. Physical death, as the "wages of sin," is only *part* of sin's penalty. What happens to the soul after it leaves the body is of even greater importance. For some, the future life will be wonderful beyond description, but it will be terrible for others. Revelation 20:14 declares that the unbelieving and wicked who are judged at the Great White Throne will be cast into the lake of fire, which is "the second death."

The opening chapters of the Bible indicate that when Adam and Eve sinned in disobedience to God, they immediately became conscious that their relationship with Him had changed. They sensed an estrangement from the Lord, so they hid themselves when they heard His voice. God had warned them not to eat of the forbidden tree, and added, ". . . for in the day that thou eatest thereof thou shalt surely die" (Genesis 2:17). They didn't fall over dead the instant they sinned, even though the seeds of physical death did begin working in their bodies. But they did die spiritually that very day. Their souls became separated from the One who had made them in His own image. They realized it and tried to hide from God when He manifested His presence in the garden. If the Lord in mercy had not called them to account, and had not forgiven and restored them, they would have gone through the rest of their earthly days in this terrible state. They would have continued dead in their sins, enemies of God. And when they died physically, they would have entered eternal death.

Every person who does not believe on Jesus Christ is now spiritually dead—separated from God. Paul said of Christians, "And you hath He made alive, *who were dead in trespasses and sins*" (Ephesians 2:1). When an unbeliever, alienated from God, undergoes physical death, he enters eternity as a child of wrath. Then, when his body is resurrected and judged at the Great White Throne, he is sent to the lake of fire, where he will experience forever what Revelation 20:14 calls "the second death." For the one who has not received Christ as Savior, then, physical death—separation of the soul from the body—is but the portent of a far more dreadful aspect of death; it is the eternal separation of the soul from God.

Death is an Enemy

The third Bible truth which helps us understand the meaning of death is found in Paul's description of it as "the last enemy" (1 Corinthians 15:26). A born-again Christian knows he has been delivered from spiritual death and understands that his soul merely leaves his body and goes to Heaven. But he still sorrows when a loved one passes on, and he has a certain amount of dread when he thinks of his own departure. This is perfectly in keeping with Paul's statement that death will continue to be the enemy of mankind until the final resurrection has taken place.

Unbelievers sometimes ridicule Christians for going to doctors when they are ill or for sorrowing when loved ones die. They say that if we really believe that going to be with Christ is so wonderful, why shouldn't we welcome an illness that might be terminal and make every funeral a festive occasion? But we need not be embarrassed by these charges. In fact, there are three reasons why it is perfectly natural and proper for us to show a certain amount of reluctance to die, and to manifest grief when people we love are taken away.

The first reason death is still an enemy is because we were not created to die. Adam was originally granted access to the tree of life, but it was denied him when he sinned. The principle of Romans 6:23 "the wages of sin is death," applies to all men. It is the God-ordained penalty for transgression.

The Bible does not give us many details about the origin of evil, but it clearly teaches that death is the result of sin. Two Old Testament passages, Isaiah 14:12-17 and Ezekiel 28:11-19, tell us that an exalted angel named Lucifer became so proud that he rebelled against God and sought to take over His throne. For this sin he was cast out of Heaven, and was assigned to the region surrounding the earth as his home and headquarters. This must have happened before God created man; maybe even before He had produced any life on our globe. This fallen angel, now called Satan, tempted Adam and Eve to disobey God, and their sin brought the penalty of death to the race.

Death is therefore a consequence of the fall. If sin had not entered our world, we would never have to see the corpse of a loved one, nor think of our own bodies as someday returning to the dust. No one would ever die.

Dying is inevitable, however, for it is the outcome of sin. It often involves suffering, and always leads to the final dissolution of the body. Yes, every time we view the remains of a loved one, we are reminded of the weakness and humiliation that is part of life because of sin. We therefore find it natural to view death as an enemy.

A second reason we have an instinctive dread of dying is that it disrupts our earthly relationships. It breaks our family ties—ties which are deep, tender, and precious. I have seen strong, vibrant, and faithful Christians who were near death begin to weep when members of their immediate family came to see them. They realized that this close relationship was about to end, and it was difficult to face. They knew they would meet again in Heaven, but that seemed so far away.

This disruptive aspect of death is also seen in the concern dying people have for a mate or dependent children. My father expressed this kind of emotion when he was taken to the hospital in serious condition. He had been blessed with unusually good health, while my mother had suffered from a serious heart ailment for years and was quite dependent upon him. The last words my father spoke shortly before he died were, "Please take good care of Mom." Yes, death is an enemy, for it disrupts relationships, tearing us away from those who need and love us.

A third reason we instinctively view death as an enemy is our natural reluctance to leave the familiar for the unfamiliar. The Bible tells us enough about Heaven to let us know that it will be a wonderful place, but it doesn't give us much information about dying and our entrance into this new realm. So, we're uneasy about the next phase of our existence. We're naturally curious about what lies ahead. This shouldn't be surprising, for we're always apprehensive in the face of something new. I remember that as a boy I was always scared when I had to start attending a new school. Even now, I am uneasy when I must do something I have never done before.

When I visited Dr. M. R. De Haan, founder of Radio Bible Class, shortly before his death, I discovered that he had a similar reaction to his impending departure. He told me that he was deeply grateful for the glorious assurance that salvation is by grace through faith, and that to be absent from the body means to be present with the Lord. Then, with a twinkle in his eye, he added, "But I wish the Lord would open the curtain just a little bit and let me take a peek at what's on the other side. I can't ask for that though, because God wants us to walk by faith."

Yes, a solemn sense of mystery hangs over death, and this gives rise to apprehension, even in the most godly. Physical death is still an enemy. It began as the result of sin, and is an intruder. It humiliates and destroys the body. It disrupts the family and terminates earthly relationships. And it involves a sense of mystery. No one should feel guilty, therefore, about showing sorrow when a loved one passes. And no one should feel he is acting inconsistently with his Christian testimony when he seeks medical help to prolong his life.

Death Can Be a Friend

The fourth biblical truth which helps give us a proper perspective of death is the clear teaching that the gain in dying far outweighs the loss for a believer. True, as we have seen, man wasn't created to die. Death has many unpleasant aspects. But the Bible assures us that when we leave this world, we immediately enter a new fellowship and blessedness which is far better than life on earth in every way.

The Old Testament saints, even though they lived many years before Christ overcame death by resurrection, were convinced that death can be a friend. They beautifully expressed their great hope of resurrection and eternal life with God. David, for example, believed that even though some wicked people prosper in this world while the righteous suffer, the final state of the godly will be more desirable by far. Speaking of life after death, he wrote, "As for me, I will behold Thy face in righteousness; I shall be satisfied, when I awake, with Thy likeness" (Psalm 17:15). David was assured that death would bring him into the state of moral perfection and complete vindication.

On some occasions the Old Testament authors spoke mournfully about dying, but they also made numerous declarations of hope and assurance. Psalm 116:15, for example, states, "Precious in the sight of the Lord is the death of His saints." The godly of those days, though ignorant of certain New Testament truths not yet revealed, often spoke of death as a friend.

The apostle Paul also believed that death can be a welcome messenger for the believer. Writing to the Christians in Philippi, he told them that he had an inner struggle whenever he thought about dying. He wanted to remain on earth and continue his ministry of building up saints and reaching sinners, but he also found within himself a yearning to be with Christ in Heaven. He was certain this would be the happier of the two possibilities, for he said, "For to me to live is Christ, and to die is gain. . . . For I am in a strait between two, having a desire to depart and to be with Christ, which is far better. Nevertheless, to abide in the flesh is more needful for you" (Philippians 1:21, 23, 24). In verse 21 he makes the statement, "To die is gain," and in verse 23 he says that being with Christ in Heaven "is far better." In my ministry I have noticed that the natural reluctance to die is usually overcome in believers who recognize that the end of life is near. The Holy Spirit apparently focuses their attention upon the glories that await them, and they look beyond the physical trauma of dying and the separation it will bring. I have seen this take place even in the lives of relatively young people who knew they were soon going to die.

Usually Christians facing death go through a patterned cycle of responses. At first they refuse to believe that they will die. Then, as their condition deteriorates, they admit they are losing the battle with disease and resign themselves to it. Up to this point, there is not much difference between the reactions of believers and unbelievers. But many Christians transcend mere resignation. They not only accept their death realistically, but look forward to it with joyous anticipation. Many have actually spoken of their eagerness to be delivered from this earthly scene with its pain, sin, and sorrow.

A pastor friend once told me of his dying brother who had lapsed into unconsciousness. The sufferer unexpectedly rallied, and opened his eyes to look into the face of his brother. He managed a slight smile and said, "Shucks! What a disappointment! I thought the next face I'd see would be that of Jesus." Many believers well along in years have told me that they felt the tug more forcefully from above than from below. After all, Jesus is in Heaven, and most of their friends have gone before, so they eagerly await their summons to come Home.

The truth that "death is gain" needs to be emphasized. It will bring comfort to the bereaved. It will minister peace to those who know that their death is imminent. It can also plant in the mind of the child of God, who may be enjoying fine health and is life-oriented, a biblical concept that will be of tremendous help in the hours of need that will inevitably come. When he must go through the valley, he will draw upon this truth already in his heart and mind, and it will bring him peace, assurance, and joy.

Summary

The Bible tells us exactly what death is: (1) Physical death is the separation of the soul from the body. (2) Spiritual death is separation from God. This is the spiritual state of every man or woman who has not accepted Jesus Christ—a condition from which people can be delivered only through faith in the Savior. When we believe in Jesus, we receive new life and are no longer alienated from God. But the person who rejects Jesus Christ and goes to his death in unbelief enters the eternal world to experience "the second death."

Death is our enemy. Our reluctance to leave this earth, therefore, and our sorrowing over the loss of loved ones are perfectly natural and proper. The Lord made us in His own image to live eternally—not to die. Death came as the consequence of sin. It tears us away from those we love. It takes us to a place we've never been. Its aura of mystery makes us afraid. But, praise God, death can be our friend! It brings deliverance from a body racked with pain. It brings release from a weariness that is almost unbearable. It brings a wonderful reunion for those who have outlived most of their friends and loved ones. And it ushers every child of God into Heaven, to be with Christ in eternal joy.

Yes, if you believe the Bible, there is *light in the valley* for you. The apostle Paul, in his last epistle, written from prison where he was awaiting execution, made this triumphant declaration: "For I am now ready to be offered, and the time of my departure is at hand. I have fought a good fight, I have finished my course, I have kept the faith; henceforth there is laid up for me a crown of righteousness, which the Lord, the righteous judge, shall give me at that day; and not to me only, but unto all them also that love His appearing" (2 Timothy 4:6-8).

Through the centuries that have followed, these great biblical truths have helped numerous Christians face death without fear. My prayer is that it will do the same for you!

2

Help
for the Dying

Some time ago I was asked to visit a lady in the hospital who had a malignant condition which was not responding to treatment. After introducing myself to her and her husband and exchanging a few casual remarks, I began talking about salvation and eternity. I was extra careful to avoid saying anything that might be taken as an indication that the lady was soon going to die. All of a sudden her husband exploded in anger and ordered me out of the room. He said that all I had talked about was death and the hereafter, and that this subject was too morbid. The wife, who had been listening intently, told him that she wanted me to continue discussing these matters. But the man was adamant, insisting that I could not pray with her or in any way make her think about her soul or eternity. At this writing, her condition is gradually worsening, but the best I have been able to do is to send her a letter and some Christian literature. The husband still refuses to allow anyone to talk to her about her spiritual condition.

This incident illustrates the unrealistic attitude many people have toward death. They do everything they can to avoid confronting this depressing subject. They won't talk about it. Some seek to escape it through drink or drugs. Others try to keep from thinking about it by a relentless pursuit of success or security, or by losing themselves in an endless search for pleasure. The popularity of horror movies and books is symptomatic of man's instinctive fear of death. Not wanting to face it rationally, he makes a macabre game of it by portraying it in gruesome stories.

Death comes to some people with no forewarning. They are suddenly taken through an automobile accident or plane crash, a massive stroke or a coronary. But many others can see their death approaching. They become ill and gradually lose ground, or else are told that they have a terminal illness and cannot recover. What can you do?

A few years ago Christian people felt free to talk openly about their departure. A husband and wife would discuss the future of the surviving partner. Words of admonition from the dying person and a touching farewell were not at all uncommon. My paternal grandparents, who both died in their late eighties, had what we used to call a "deathbed." I was in my teens at the time, and I vividly recall walking into the room and saying goodby. I still remember their telling me to live for God and His glory. One of my uncles had prepared a long list of admonitions and instructions for his family, and he presented it to them when they gathered by his bed. Dr. M. R. De Haan, founder of the Radio Bible Class, gave final words of counsel to his grandchildren, and offered a moving prayer on their behalf before he went home to Glory.

What a striking contrast to many of the situations I have encountered as a pastor! Sometimes people want to hide the truth from a dying loved one. A number of times I have been told, "Don't let him know what the doctor said. He'll just give up." I look back with regret upon a time I co-operated with a father and mother when their teenage son was dying. He was slowly wasting away, but they insisted that I talk with him as if he would get well again. Finally, he slipped into a coma and died. I'm thankful that he was a Christian, but now I wish we had been honest with him. I don't know to this day whether or not he really knew that he was dying. Much needless suffering is endured when a person suspects that he's going to die, and his loved ones know it, but no one dares to talk about it.

Christians should be truthful in all matters, and this includes letting a person know when the doctors say he has no hope for recovery. When we bring it into the open, it's easier for everybody. The patient will then be able to experience the marvel of God's special dying grace. The family will have some very precious times of fellowship and will be able to look back upon the Homegoing of their loved one as a spiritually victorious event. And those who observe it will see what Christ can do to make death beautiful and how He comforts His children.

While some Christians readily accept the announcement that their illness is terminal, this isn't true of everyone. I have seen some believers go through an intense emotional struggle when confronted with this information. It shouldn't really surprise us, for a reluctance to die is natural. But we should also know that most born-again people finally reach the place of calm acceptance or even thrilling expectation. In this chapter, therefore, I will discuss the emotions people go through when they realize their death is near. My purpose is twofold: (1) to help those facing death to understand their feelings, and (2) to show Christians how they can help the dying.

Dr. Elisabeth Kübler-Ross, a psychiatrist who specializes in counseling with the terminally ill and their families, lists five emotional stages through which a person often passes when he knows the end is near. They are: (1) denial, (2) resentment, (3) bargaining, (4) depression, and (5) acceptance. Not everyone passes through all of these stages, of course, nor can one always clearly mark off a specific time when one stage is left and the next entered. It's helpful, however, to have some idea of how people facing death usually react when made aware of their condition.

Denial

The initial response to the news of one's impending death is often denial. The patient is likely to tell you he doesn't believe he's going to die. He might insist that a mistake has been made in diagnosis. Or he may simply say, "They told me I'm going to die, but I know it can't be true. I'm going to get well. Just wait and see." I used to think this kind of talk was only an effort to keep up hope, but I've now concluded that the patient really doesn't believe it's going to happen to him. He realizes that death does come to people in every age bracket, but he just can't believe it's happening to him. Meanwhile, all the time he's denying it, he's really making an inner adjustment to it.

To help someone in this state of mind, you should be extremely tactful. It would be unwise to encourage him with false hopes, or to upset him by insisting that he's wrong. Listen to him patiently. Assure him that you'd like to have him get well. If you pray with him, ask the Lord for healing if that is His will, but also request that God will provide special grace if He is not going to bring recovery. This will reassure the dying person of your genuine concern, and demonstrate your implicit faith in God's goodness.

Resentment

The period of denial may be followed by a time of resentment or anger. The dying person is finally convinced that the doctors are right, but he wonders why he's the victim. He knows that many people his age are still healthy and looking forward to the future, but he's almost finished. It doesn't seem fair. If he's not a believer, he may curse his tough luck and take it out on his family and friends. He may blame the doctor for being too slow in making the diagnosis. In a vague way he's mad at the whole world for what's happening to him, and he shows it.

Just because the patient is a Christian is no guarantee that he will not go through the same period of resentment. He may make it unpleasant for his family and the people trying to help him. I remember that when we thought mother was about to die (though she recovered and lived another 12 years), she felt some bitterness. She told me it just didn't seem fair that she should depart before she could enjoy her grandchildren. She had raised a large family through the depression years, and just when life was becoming easier and money was a bit more plentiful, it looked as if she was going to have to leave. She had too much reverence for God to express defiance or anger, but she did go through a brief period of resentment.

When we are trying to help a person who is in this mood, we must be careful not to reinforce his negative feelings. We should not dwell upon the thought that the doctor may have been negligent or incompetent, nor encourage the patient in his complaining. Some Christian counselors say it's healthy for the terminally ill to express their bitterness or anger, but I don't agree. Even though this may be a natural reaction, it is not right.

I sometimes have responded to resentful people by saying something like this: "I think I understand how you feel, and I'm quite sure that if I were in your situation I wouldn't react any differently. Yet both of us know that God doesn't make mistakes, and that He is working out a plan for your eternal good. I realize that it's easier for me to say this as I stand here at your bedside than it would be for you, but it's true nevertheless. And I'm sure that God, who knows our human frailty, understands and forgives you." When praying with a person in this stage of reaction, I try to be brief and direct, avoiding anything that might sound like preaching.

Bargaining

The third stage the person who is dying may go through is that of bargaining. He begins to barter for an extension of the time he has left. He may say, for example, "I'll be satisfied if I can live long enough to see my youngest daughter graduate from high school"; or, "If I can just live to see my first grandchild, I'll be happy." He is likely to try to make a deal with God. One man, who had been dishonest in his business practices and spasmodic in church attendance, thought he was dying and called for me to come and see him. He confessed his wrongs and declared that he would be different if God would only give him a few extra years. He even asked me to pray for an extension of his life, earnestly assuring me of his sincerity. Most people are not this open about their bargaining. But many will make a secret pact with the Lord, promising changes if He will give them a little more time.

If one of our loved ones or friends is in this emotional stage, he needs a good listener more than anything else. Let him talk about the things he'd like to do. If he's well enough to go for a ride, by all means take him. Let him squeeze out of life whatever enjoyment he can still get, but don't be dishonest with him. Don't say he's going to keep on living for a number of years when you are almost certain that it's only a matter of weeks or months. The patient needs a friend who can be completely natural with him. If he wants to watch a football game on TV, let him do it without feelings of guilt. He has accepted the fact that he's going to die soon, but he's hoping that this interim can be extended for just a little longer than the doctors expect. He wants to enjoy the legitimate pleasures of this life as long as he can, and we should let him. Please—no lectures or pious platitudes!

Depression

The fourth stage the terminally ill person goes through is depression. He has now accepted the verdict that he's soon going to die, and he's thinking about the end rather than the intervening time. He isn't happy about the prospect. The elements of fear and disappointment, coupled with a feeling of loneliness, bring on deep depression. Quite often he doesn't want to talk, doesn't feel like eating, and may turn his face to the wall when you come to see him. He may like to sleep as much as he can, because it's the only way he can get away from his gloom and melancholy.

When someone is in this state of depression, we must remember that he is grieving as he works his way toward acceptance. Don't stay away from him just because he isn't talking. He desperately needs to know that people care. Members of his family should be with him as much as possible. It's all right to converse among yourselves if he seems to have tuned everybody out. You are helping him just by being there. Little acts of kindness like getting him a glass of cold water or making him more comfortable are deeply appreciated. So are words and physical tokens of affection. A kiss from a loved one or a gentle squeeze of the hand can do much to help the sufferer through this difficult time.

It's a mistake to enter a dying person's room and try to generate an atmosphere of artificial gaiety. People sometimes do this because they're nervous and uncomfortable, but all efforts at slapstick humor are definitely out of place. It's not the time for boisterous laughter or corny jokes. A few quietly spoken words and little tokens of concern will do far more than you might ever realize.

Acceptance

The final emotional stage of the person who knows he's going to die is that of acceptance. This term used by Dr. Kübler-Ross doesn't adequately indicate the difference between the attitude of the non-believer toward his death and that of the mature, yielded Christian. It's one thing to submit to the unavoidable, but it's quite another to be joyful in anticipation.

When the non-Christian reaches the place of

calm acceptance, he usually becomes withdrawn and takes very little interest in things around him. He doesn't really have very much to talk about, because he has no certain hope for what lies beyond. Though vaguely fearful, he is resigned to the inevitable.

If the dying person is a believer, we can help him move on from calm acceptance to joyful expectation. We can do this by talking openly and frankly about the spiritual realities of our faith. I have had delightful times at the bedsides of people who knew they were dying, and I have seen them remarkably free from discomfort when we discussed the wonder of salvation by grace and the glory of the place He has prepared for us.

On one occasion, a few sentences I spoke brought about a tremendous change in the attitude of a young woman who knew that she had less than a month to live. She had sent word requesting that I see her, and I found her calm and composed. She had already passed through the time of resentment and bargaining. She truly believed that her sins were forgiven and that she possessed eternal life. But she was still troubled, wondering why God would take her from her husband and three small children when they needed her so badly.

What I said was not profound. Any believer could have given the same answer. As nearly as I remember, I said, "Mary, I can't tell you exactly why the Lord is taking you Home right now. Believe me, if I had my way, you would remain here with your husband and children. But I am convinced that if you and I knew everything God knows, we would agree that His way is best. You can be sure that He loves your children even more than you do, and that He has a plan for their care. The moment after you die you will be supremely happy, and it will seem like no time at all before you'll meet again the people you have left behind. I will see you too, and we'll probably smile as we remember how we were inclined to worry about tomorrow and to put so much value upon a few extra years of life on earth." We talked for another 10 or 15 minutes, and then I read a brief passage of Scripture and prayed with her. The Holy Spirit used these few words to lift her from a position of mere resignation to one of praise to the Lord for His goodness and grace.

I have a deep conviction that people should be told the truth when they have a terminal condition. Let's have an end to this business of being deceitful. A dying person often knows what's happening to him, but somehow he can't bring himself to say anything about it. His loved ones likewise realize that he will soon be leaving them, and they wonder if he suspects anything. They put on an air of cheerfulness and make small talk in an effort to cover up the true situation. How much easier it would be for everyone concerned if people were willing to discuss the truth freely and openly.

A Christian who knows the end is near will make his emotional adjustment readily. As family and friends of the patient, you can be tremendously helpful, mainly by showing him that you love him, by staying near him, and by making him as comfortable as possible. It will be thrilling to observe the change in the person you love as he waits for his summons to "come up higher." And when he dies, you will have precious memories to ponder and the bright prospect of reunion to cherish. This will soften the sorrow of bereavement. Yes, honesty at the time of approaching death is best for everyone. It helps the dying one adjust to his imminent departure, and makes it easier for his loved ones to endure the grief.

3

How to Handle
Your Fear

I know people who are afraid to talk about death.
I've seen men and women become terror-stricken
when they heard that their illness was incurable.
I recently saw a man begin to tremble, break into
sobs, and then flail his arms wildly when he was
told that his malignancy was beyond treatment.
My heart went out to him as I stood beside his
bed and tried to comfort him. I could understand
why he was afraid. He had grown up in a Christian
home, but had never made an open profession of
faith in Jesus Christ. He had dropped out of
church and had lived a selfish, worldly life. Now
he was suddenly faced with death, and it terrified
him. He was afraid of the judgment to come. He
was worried about the pain and distress he might
endure in dying. I'm glad to say that before his
death he found peace with God through faith in
Christ, but I shall never forget the moment he received the news. He was just plain scared.

All of us contemplate death with a degree of
apprehension. But the Bible gives us much infor-

mation that will help assuage our anxieties. I pray that the light of God's Word will dispel the gloom that naturally surrounds those who are facing the end of their earthly life and separation from their loved ones. Only the Lord can help us pass through the valley that lies before us with untroubled and hope-filled hearts.

The Fear of Punishment or Shame

A major cause for fearing death is a concern about being punished for sin, or being ashamed of the way we've lived. This is true even though our society is primarily materialistic and lives only for the present. Naturalistic evolution is taught as if it were a scientifically proven fact, but most people still believe in some kind of Supreme Being, and they worry about judgment for sin. The current interest in astrology, spiritism, and other forms of the occult demonstrates that people in general are not really convinced that death ends everything.

A secular report recently stated that death is faced with more composure by outright atheists and committed Christians than by people who have never had strong convictions in either direction. It pointed out that the dogmatic atheist has conditioned himself to accept the idea of extinction, and so meets his last enemy with stoicism and raw courage. It also acknowledged that many sincere Christians die with an attitude of joy and expectation. In fact, many believers have spoken of hearing Heaven's music and catching a glimpse of its glory just before they expired, and these observations are mentioned by some non-believers who have done research on the process of dying. They maintain, of course, that the person is having hallucinations or is in a state of euphoria, but they cannot prove this evaluation. I personally see no reason to doubt the reality of these experiences, and I'm glad these scientists do recognize that many Christians find death to be a beautiful event.

Those who fear punishment or shame after death are usually either halfhearted Christians or people with only a vague belief in God. But even unbelievers and agnostics are not free from anxieties. They can't always convince themselves that death really ends everything.

One young man who had claimed to be an infidel became snowbound and died in a cabin somewhere in Canada. When they found his body, they discovered a note addressed to his mother which said, "As I think of dying, the thought that plagues me is not whether or not there is a God, but how can I stand before Him in all my sin." Yes, the fear of punishment can be very real. People can push it aside by telling themselves that they are not worse than the average, and may even rationalize that their good deeds will outweigh their bad. But down deep inside, they are apprehensive.

As noted earlier, even some true Christians are fearful. They are afraid of what will happen when they stand before Christ. One man, who had been active in church work but had always been somewhat proud and sensual, was distraught when he realized he was dying. He wept as he told me that he dreaded the judgment seat of Christ. This is not uncommon among believers who have been selfish and disobedient to the Lord.

If you are called upon to minister to a non-Christian, keep in mind that you must not deviate from the truth to make him less afraid. It's sinful to offer him false assurance. He must be warned about the reality of judgment, and the message of salvation should be explained to him as clearly as possible. He can still be saved. I have had the joy of leading people to Christ just before they died. In each case much prayer had been offered for them by their loved ones. I vividly recall that after the funeral of a man who had accepted Christ a few months before he died, a woman came to me with tears in her eyes and said, "I am Gerrit's cousin, and I'm as grateful and happy as I can be! I was with his mother when she died, and her last words were a prayer for the Lord to save her wayward son."

That illustration should not give you the wrong impression. Though some people are born again in the midnight hour, the vast majority are not. People who have repeatedly heard the message of salvation, and yet have continued to reject it will seldom be inclined to believe it when they're about to die. They may be afraid, but somehow their hearts have been hardened to the truth, and they refuse it. If you see this attitude in a friend or member of your family, you will be deeply moved, but don't become angry with him or desert him. Remain faithful to your responsibility and continue to show the love of Christ. Your part is to prepare the soil and sow the seed of the truth through the way you live and witness. The Lord alone can bring the harvest.

When you encounter a Christian who is afraid of meeting the Lord Jesus because of the carnal and self-centered way he has lived, encourage him by reminding him that salvation is by grace alone. Don't minimize his failures or try to whitewash his sins, but emphasize the fact that all of us are unprofitable servants. I personally find it easy to identify with such a person because I see in my own life so much selfishness and pride. Sometimes I feel a sense of shame as I contemplate standing before my Lord, the One who knows everything about me. How true the words of Lamentations 3:22, "It is because of the Lord's mercies that we are not consumed, because His compassions fail not." How comforting to know that Jesus Christ took ALL the punishment for our sins, and that there is nothing left for us to pay! I'm sure that even the very best of us will be ashamed of some elements in our lives when we stand before Christ. But the blessedness of being accepted in His presence through grace alone will far outweigh our feelings of embarrassment or humiliation.

The Fear of the Death Struggle

Many are afraid of the actual physical distress that may accompany the dying moment. An aged man in the hospital put it rather eloquently when he said, "I know I'm going to die soon, and I'm just a bit afraid. I have complete confidence when I view the other side of the river, but it's getting across that frightens me." Many have expressed a similar feeling. Our bodies are very much a part of us, and sometimes a real struggle is involved when death occurs. It's only natural to feel some dread of this experience.

It should help all of us to realize that God has made the physical part of dying easier than it may appear. He has built in certain factors which greatly minimize the distress. Doctors say that the accumulation of carbon dioxide in the blood has a euphoric effect. Then, too, a person often is not conscious of physical pain, even though he may appear to be enduring great agony. One of my friends, who had been strapped down because of the way he was thrashing about with a raging fever, said later that he had no recollection of pain during this time; he had only a feeling of great peace and tranquillity. Apparently the nervous system responds to physical stimuli even though the mind does not register it.

When a Christian consciously trusts in God for help in his dying hours, the Lord often seems to give an inner joy which makes him unaware of his physical discomfort. I have often observed that trusting believers are remarkably free from pain, and are even able to rejoice in the Lord when one would expect them to be enduring intense anguish. Recently I went to a rest home to see a man who had been very kind to me in my youth. He had been bedridden for some 4 years, and his physical condition had deteriorated to a deplorable state. I thought he would be in agony, but he was remarkably comfortable. I wish everyone who is worried about dying could have seen his smile and heard his testimony. One of his nurses told me, "He makes it easy to believe in Jesus Christ."

Christian friend, don't be afraid of dying. Why worry and rob yourself of the joy and peace the Lord wants you to have right now? A lady I once knew was morbidly fearful of hospitals, and continually asked people to pray that she would have "dying grace." But when she became ill and her condition was beyond help, she accepted the news calmly. Then, a couple of days before her Homegoing, she looked up at her loved ones and smiled as she said, "So this is what I've been dreading all my life! It isn't anything like I thought it would be. How foolish was all my worrying!"

The Fear of Alienation

A third anxiety experienced by dying people is the feeling of aloneness that gradually develops. The patient is on his way out of this world, and that seems to separate him from his loved ones and friends. They are all life-oriented and busy, but he's going to die. He knows that one of these days he'll be gone, and they'll all go back to their activities almost as if nothing significant has happened. These thoughts bring a feeling of estrangement to the dying person, and make him lonely and afraid.

Loved ones and friends can help the terminal patient overcome this fear by being with him as much as possible. He needs to know they still feel close to him, and that they are reluctant to see him leave. A member of the family should never come in and say he can stay for only a few minutes because he has some pressing duties. If this occurs repeatedly, the patient will soon think you don't care to be with him anymore. You must be careful that you don't begin to separate yourself from him before death completes the job. Joseph Bayly tells of a man who was unintentionally hurt by his wife's actions. When he was first hospitalized, she kissed him on the lips whenever she left him. Then later on she kissed him on the forehead, and finally she was merely blowing kisses to him from the doorway. The dying person knows he's going to leave his family, but he must never be allowed to feel that they are already starting to leave him.

This fear of alienation sometimes causes the patient to think he will be forgotten soon after he dies. Dying people have often told me that they know they will hardly be missed. To some extent, of course, this is true, for even famous men and women do not remain in our minds forever. But everyone needs the assurance that his life meant something to his family and friends. He must believe that someone is going to miss him after he goes, and wish that he were still around. Even non-Christian counselors, though they have no confidence in a coming resurrection and reunion in Heaven, will do their best to assure a dying person that his life was not in vain. I believe that we who know the Lord can help the dying by reminiscing with them when they want to talk about the past. It may be well to bring to the mind of the patient some of the good things he has done and some of the ways he has helped you. This lets him know that his life has had some significance and meaning, and stimulates his anticipation of the day when he and all his Christian loved ones will be reunited in Heaven.

The glorious spiritual truth that no one who believes in Christ dies alone is a tremendous comfort. This biblical promise has been proven true in the experience of millions. Countless believers have been comforted and strengthened by the words, "Yea, though I walk through the valley of the shadow of death, I will fear no evil; *for Thou art with me*" (Psalm 23:4). G. Campbell Morgan once read these words to an aged lady, ". . . lo, I am with you always, even unto the end of the age" (Matthew 28:20). He then commented, "That's a wonderful promise!" With a twinkle in her eye she corrected him, saying, "That's more than a promise, it's a present reality."

I vividly recall, as a young boy in a Sunday morning service, hearing an elderly, white-haired seminary professor say with great feeling, "I've gone through all the wonderful and exciting stages of human life from the cradle to old age. Now I can only look forward to taking that journey, that last journey, which everyone walks alone. Yet I won't really be alone. The Lord Jesus has assured me that He will be with me, and I believe Him. I have sensed His presence in times of joy and gladness, in times of sorrow and pain. I therefore have every confidence that He will be my companion when I go through that dark valley which leads to my eternal Home." Yes, God has made provision for that final moment. No believer needs to be afraid of being alone when he takes that step where earthly friends cannot go with him. Jesus will be there.

Other Fears

A number of other vague fears are connected with thoughts of dying: What if I become a burden? Will I become incoherent and act foolishly? Will I become a horrid spectacle through the ravages of some disease?

I would not deny that thoughts like these may arise. But a Christian should not dwell upon them, nor let them throw him into a state of depression. We must never forget that we are in the hands of God who loves us and has a good purpose in everything He permits to come into our lives. Furthermore, we don't begrudge the time we must spend with one of our loved ones who is dying. We therefore have good reason to believe that those who love us will likewise care for us, and will not look upon us as a burden if we should become helpless.

The fear of humiliation—of losing our dignity either through mental confusion, total helplessness, or physical deterioration—can be largely eliminated if we remind ourselves that real beauty comes from within. Our resurrection bodies will be perfect, untouched by the effects of disease or injury. Paul said that he was not discouraged, even though his body was wasting away, because his spirit was being renewed day by day while he gazed upon the spiritual and eternal rather than the things of time (see 2 Corinthians 4:16-18). Remember, in 1 Corinthians 10:13 God promised that He will not permit any test to come into our lives without giving us all that we need to endure and overcome it.

Just before a man went to the hospital for an operation, which at best would extend his life for only a brief period of time, he said to me, "Brother, I want to tell you right now that I have complete faith in Jesus Christ, and that I have no fear of death. I believe He died for my sins and that He rose from the grave. I don't know what's going to happen to me. I may die by inches, and in the process become delirious and say things I don't really mean. That's why I'm telling you now that if I ever say anything different, don't believe me. And just remember that if I die, you'll have nothing on me. The Bible says that the dead in Christ shall rise first."

Yes, there are fears connected with dying, and even the most devout believers experience them. But through the ministry of brothers and sisters in Christ and the blessed Spirit of God, no believer need go out of this world with either the whimper of a frightened baby or the grim, determined look of the atheist. He can die victoriously and triumphantly in Christ.

4

Coping
with Grief

Sometimes the grief that comes to us when a loved one dies is almost more than we can bear. Sorrow takes different forms with different people, and is therefore difficult to describe. Gladys Hunt speaks of it as "a smothery feeling." Robert J. Vetter, a dynamic Christian executive, said that when his young, talented wife died unexpectedly, at first his stomach was in knots and his "insides churned as though a violent virus had knocked me down." C. S. Lewis, who had remained a bachelor until middle age and then was very happily married, lost his beloved wife after a brief bout with cancer. In his book *A Grief Observed*, he said that when she died, and for some time afterward, he had a fluttering sensation in his stomach much like that of terrible fear, and that for some reason he had to keep swallowing. Others have spoken of the feelings of loneliness, helplessness, guilt, and anger that swept over them like huge, crashing ocean waves. No two people have exactly the same feelings at a time of bereavement.

In addition, we all express our grief in different ways. Some may weep openly when a death occurs, and shed many tears. Others don't let themselves show emotion in public, and cry very little even when they're alone. Some talk freely, expressing their sorrow or guilt or anger both to friends and to God; others keep everything bottled up inside. I have seen people scream out their initial resentment toward God, then later adopt a beautiful spirit of submission to His will. And I have seen some maintain their outward composure throughout the first few days, then fall apart afterward because of their bitterness and unwillingness to accept the difficult experience God allowed to come into their lives.

The Lord expects us to feel and express sorrow when a loved one dies, but He does not want us to be completely overwhelmed with grief. We dishonor Him when we lose all interest in life, become mired in self-pity, or act as if death were the end of everything. The Old Testament patriarchs buried their dead and went on with the affairs of life. When David learned that his handsome son Absalom had been killed in a revolt, he wanted to retreat from his duties as king of Israel. But he accepted a rebuke from his general and began again to fulfill the task God had given him. The apostle Paul said that although believers in Christ do sorrow, their grief is not like that of others who have no hope (see 1 Thessalonians 4:13). In a time of bereavement, therefore, Christians should exercise self-control, and submit to the healing power of "Gilead's balm." Even while expressing our sorrow, our relatives and friends should be able to see that we have the help of God and the assurance of eternal life in Heaven.

This chapter has been written to help you learn

how to cope with your grief as a believer. I am convinced that we ought to prepare ourselves beforehand for the coming hour of sorrow, and that this can best be done by a daily life of faith and obedience. After all, you know that death will strike your family sometime, and the closer you walk with the Lord in days of sunshine, the greater will be the reality of His presence when you go through the valley of sorrow. When a loved one dies, you will be able to bear your grief less painfully if you will follow these three imperatives: (1) Believe God's truth about death. (2) Express your feelings. (3) Maintain a true perspective.

Believe God's Truth

The first way a person who is grieving over the death of a loved one can cope with his feelings is to bring to his mind the biblical teaching about death and to believe it. It may seem that I'm saying the obvious when I tell a Christian—one who has already confessed his faith in Christ and affirmed his confidence in the resurrection—that he should believe God's Word. Doesn't every Christian believe? Yes, but at a time of death, our emotions tend to take control of us, and we may forget the basic tenets of our faith.

This very thing happened to an aged Christian woman whose husband was suddenly taken from her. She kept saying over and over, "Poor man! Poor man! I feel so sorry for him." She then would sob uncontrollably, and her relatives were at a loss to know how to calm her down. As her pastor, I thought she was indulging in self-pity, and believed she was unconsciously trying to impress us with how much she had loved her husband. I therefore said quite sternly, "Mrs. Shultz, you're acting as if there is no God. Your husband is not to be pitied, for he is with the Lord. You're going to see him again, and God is going to take care of you until He calls you Home. You are denying what you really believe by the things you are saying and the way you are acting." She was shocked by these blunt words, but she recognized that what I said was true. From that point on she began to show more trust in God.

As Christians we entered our new life by believing Jesus Christ, and faith is also to be the pre-eminent characteristic of our daily walk. The life that pleases God is one of implicit trust in Him. How important, therefore, that we affirm what we believe when we are called upon to go through the most difficult of all human experiences—the death of a loved one.

It will be easier to exercise faith in a time of bereavement if we walk with the Lord day by day, and always take seriously the promises and commands of the Bible. I can testify that this is true from my own experience. Every time I have had to look upon the body of a believing loved one in a casket, I have found myself actually rejoicing through my tears. The separation and humiliation of death does cause sorrow, but when we realize that the soul has gone to Heaven, and that the body will be resurrected and given a glory beyond our imagination, we feel a thrill of joy and expectation.

When I was a little boy, my parents bought a small life insurance policy for each member of the family. As I overheard them talking with the agent about death payments, I told myself that I just couldn't stand it if mom or dad or one of my brothers should die. But my fears were unjustified. When the time came for the departure of my parents and two of my brothers, I found a comfort

I hadn't dreamed possible. I was actually happy as I reflected upon their blessedness in being with the Lord, and the glorious reunion we're going to have someday in Heaven. Yes, if you pray regularly and read the Scriptures daily, it will be easier to reaffirm your faith in a time of sorrow. And when you do, your heart will be filled with joy and peace.

Express Your Feelings

The second imperative to be obeyed in a time of grief is, "Express your feelings." We mentioned earlier that our emotions sometimes seem to overwhelm us when someone we love dies. We may experience deep feelings of guilt about things we said or did, or things we failed to do. We find ourselves saying, "How I wish I had another chance to show him how much I love him!" We may be so engulfed with loneliness or so afraid of the future that we wish we could die too. Bitter thoughts may also well up within us—anger at what God has done to us or resentment against the ways of His providence. We may even admit to ourselves that these thoughts are sinful, but somehow we are unable to control them.

When this occurs, we need to express our thoughts to God. We must tell Him exactly how we feel, asking Him for forgiveness and help. It may even be wise to confide in someone we trust who has spiritual discernment, and ask him to pray for and with us. A flesh-and-blood human being who is willing to identify with us, and then assures us that God understands and forgives, can be of inestimable value at such a time. Christian friend, don't bottle up those bitter, angry thoughts and feelings. They need to be expressed to God, and maybe to your pastor or a friend. And as you talk about them, you'll find them beginning to disappear, as God ministers to your sorrowing heart.

Maintain a True Perspective

The third command to one who is going through a period of sorrow is, "Maintain a true perspective." This means that we should analyze the effect our grief is having upon us. God has given each of us a will and a mind as well as emotions, and He expects us to use them. Sober reflection and appraisal will enable us to see that our deep hurt is clouding our perspective and dulling our senses. We will recognize that our feelings of guilt, helplessness, and fear of the future are magnified out of proportion to the real situation. It's like thinking about our problems when we're tired. They tend to look like mountains at nighttime, but in the morning they are far less foreboding. Remember, the strain that accompanies death produces a weariness that keeps us from seeing the true picture. But when we realize that grief has a way of blurring our vision, and we ask the indwelling Holy Spirit to keep us in touch with spiritual reality, He will help us maintain a proper outlook.

When we see the situation from the biblical viewpoint, we will have reason for thanksgiving even in our sorrow. We may not feel like giving thanks for the death that occurred, but we can find many things for which to be grateful. A minister said he just couldn't thank God for the auto accident that killed his 24-year-old son, but he still had much reason for thanksgiving. He and his wife had many precious memories of their boy, a host of wonderful Christian friends to support them, a Bible full of promises, and a glorious hope of reunion with their loved one in Heaven.

My friend, when you honestly appraise your

grief, and see how it distorts reality, you will begin to see clearly again. You'll once more view life as worthwhile, and conclude that there still are many reasons for going on. A mother who has lost a child, for example, will be able to come out of the shell of sorrow she has pulled around herself. She will resume her duties and responsibilities toward her husband and her other children. A widow will think of all the good things in her life, and begin helping others in worse circumstances than her own. Yes, when you see the future from the vantage point of faith, you will not be paralyzed by fear or think life isn't worth the living.

Conclusion

When a death occurs, Christian men and women have no right to act as if there is no God who cares. The Lord expects His children to exercise their faith, to be honest in their relationship with Him, to look to Him for help, and to face reality in the light of scriptural truth. It's a matter of consciously trusting God—of applying to life the truths taught in His Word.

I know that Christians *can* be victorious and triumphant in a time of bereavement. I've seen it happen time and time again. On one occasion, I was conducting the service of committal in a cemetery, when suddenly the father of the 20-year-old girl who had been asphyxiated began to sing the Doxology. The family joined him in this song of praise, and I could see in their faces that it was real to them. They believed God and were experiencing His presence and comfort.

What a contrast to what I have observed among those who do not know the Lord Jesus! I have looked at the faces of non-believers and seen only hopelessness and despair. I've watched them even talk to the dead body, because it's all they had left. I'll never forget the pathetic words of a man in his thirties standing at the open casket as the family came to pay their last respects. He said, "Goodby, Dad." He then murmured, "We'll never see you again."

If you know the Lord Jesus, you need not sorrow like this. You can be triumphant! And you should be!

5

Helping
the Bereaved

The sorrow of bereavement can be made easier
to bear by the understanding words and thought-
ful actions of fellow-believers. I have certainly
found this to be true in my own experience. And
many people have said to me at the time of grief,
"I never knew until now how wonderful it is to
have Christian friends. They've been such a help
and comfort to me!"

But I must also admit regretfully that God's
people don't always show the sympathy they
should. Often men or women who have lost a
loved one have asked me, "What's the matter with
the people of my church? What's wrong with my
relatives? Ever since the funeral, no one comes to
see me anymore." I usually try to make excuses,
pointing out that life today is busy, and that most
of us can't do everything we wish we could. But
down in my heart I know I'm copping out. The
real trouble is that we are too self-centered to
share another's grief. We need to start taking
more seriously such biblical commands as, "Bear

ye one another's burdens, and so fulfill the law of Christ" (Galatians 6:2), and ". . . weep with them that weep" (Romans 12:15).

I'm sure you'll agree that we do sometimes fail to be as kind and considerate to the sorrowing as we ought to be. And most of us feel guilty about the way we've neglected someone we love, but we don't know what to do about it. We're afraid we'll say the wrong thing and do more harm than good. This chapter will help you to be successful in fulfilling your Christian responsibility, for it tells how to comfort the bereaved. I will give you five guidelines to follow if you want to be effective in the ministry of compassion.

Pray for the Grieving

Our efforts to comfort the sorrowing must begin with prayer, for in the final analysis only God can heal the wounds of grief. For this reason the Scriptures call us to a ministry of intercession for others, and such prayer is indeed effective. In my pastoral ministry, numerous people have told me that in their darkest hours of bereavement they were experiencing a unique consciousness of the Lord's presence and help. They said they knew it could be attributed only to the faithful prayers of friends and relatives.

The death of one very close to us may leave us so numbed by grief that it's difficult even to think, much less to pray intelligently. This is when we urgently need, in addition to the conscious exercise of our own faith, the intercessory ministry of others. That's why in a time of great sorrow we find ourselves saying, "Please pray for me." Yes, the most wonderful thing we can do for a sorrowing friend is to pray for him.

Express Your Sympathy

The second guideline for ministering to the grieving is, "Express your sympathy." The emphasis is upon the word "express." Speak to the sorrowing, or write them if it's impossible to see them in person. You may be deeply moved by the sorrow that has come into the life of someone you know, but you will not help him unless you communicate your feelings. I realize that this is often difficult to do. We tend to shy away from visiting those who have experienced terrible tragedy because we wonder what we ought to say. So we avoid seeing them, and don't do anything.

Gladys Hunt, in her book *Don't Be Afraid to Die*, gives an example of how natural it is for us to fail in expressing our feelings to the bereaved. A little boy had died from a rare disease, and the news immediately reached the neighborhood. They had all gathered in small groups to talk about it, when the parents of the little boy suddenly drove down the street and turned into their driveway. Conversation immediately ceased. Parents picked up their small children and hastened into the house. Only one couple had the grace to walk over to the grieving parents and say, "I'm so sorry." It wasn't that the other people on the street were calloused or unkind. They just didn't know what to say. Besides, some of them almost felt as if they should apologize for having children who hadn't died. These are natural human reactions. But how foolish! The sight of other children wouldn't have caused the grieving parents to feel cheated because their child had been taken. But they would have appreciated an understanding word from all their neighbors. The failure of these friends made for an awkward situation and actually compounded the grief of the people who had lost their little boy.

Avoiding the grieving person is never the right thing to do. A young couple might be reluctant to express their sympathy to a woman in their own age bracket who has lost her husband, thinking that when she sees the two of them together, it will bring a painful reminder of her loss. But that just isn't true. The bereaved woman will be comforted greatly by knowing that you care enough to try to console her. She will appreciate your effort, as well as your continuing friendship.

Yes, *expressing* your sympathy really helps the sorrowing. It removes the awkwardness from your next meeting with that person. And it opens the door to ongoing fellowship.

Let Your Words Be Few

The third rule for ministering to the grieving is, "Let your words be few." Don't make the mistake of trying to say too much. The person who is sorrowing is not in the mood for a long speech. He won't appreciate a series of pious sentiments or a string of religious clichés. At the funeral home I have often seen someone monopolize the sorrowing person for a long period of time, when it was obvious that the bereaved was only enduring the monologue and receiving no benefit whatever.

When you talk too much, you are always in danger of being offensive. This is no time to say things which are intended to minimize the hurt, but might be taken wrongly. Don't say something like, "You'll be surprised at how quickly you'll adjust to your new way of life." The person isn't ready for this yet. Nor is it wise to speak reprovingly, "You're taking it too hard. Just think of all the blessings you still have." What you're saying may be true, and at times a pastor or someone very close to the bereaved person may find it necessary to jar him out of his self-pity. But normally it's cruel to tell someone that he is grieving too much, for it seems to be an indication that you think he is placing too much value upon the one who has departed. Nor does he want to hear that he'll soon become accustomed to being without that loved one. He may get the idea that you don't think the one who has gone was very important.

It's best to express yourself in few words when you see the grieving person the first time. A simple "I'm sorry" or "We're praying for you" is always appropriate. And it helps. If you're in the funeral home, avoid commenting about the appearance of the deceased. To do so is to draw attention to the shell that remains after death, when the emphasis should be placed upon the blessedness of his being with Christ. Of course, if a member of the family says something about how natural the loved one looks, we're not to be technical and point out that it's only the body. Express simple agreement.

After the funeral you may have opportunity to engage in extended conversation with the one who has been bereaved. Let him or her take the lead. Join in the reminiscing and feel free to add to the positive memories. But above everything else, be a good listener. We err far more in saying too much than too little.

Remember the Children

When a death occurs, we must not forget that the children need comfort too. Sometimes people, seeing a child absorbed in play, think he doesn't feel deep grief. This is a mistake. The great Bible teacher G. Campbell Morgan said that when his sister died, he was just a small boy; yet he often went to her grave and wept.

If you are called upon to tell a child that a

loved one has died, be honest with him. I have seen well-meaning people hide the truth, saying something like, "Daddy is going to be gone for a while." Then they don't permit the children to see the body, and this gives the youngsters the idea that their father will come back sometime. They eventually do come to understand that he won't return, but they also realize that someone they trusted very much didn't tell them the whole truth. This in turn could make them doubt what they are told about other important matters like God and salvation.

I also believe we should let the child know what death really is. If we say that his loved one has gone to be with Jesus, but don't explain anything about the body being left behind, the youngster will have serious misconceptions. He will picture the whole person floating heavenward. One of my nieces was about three years old when her little cousin died. The parents came home from viewing the body of the baby and spoke of how pretty she was. This puzzled the youngster, and she asked, "Hasn't she gone up yet?" We should try to prevent such mistaken notions right from the start.

You may wonder how truthful we should be in explaining death to children, for fear that the thought of the dissolution of the body is too gruesome for them to handle. I don't think it is. Children at a very young age are often quite realistic about death. They've had their pets die, or heard their friends talk about a grandparent who passed away. They take these things in stride—sometimes better than we do. They are amazingly resilient. It's especially important to place the emphasis upon the soul going to be with God. The simplicity of a child's faith enables him to believe in the blessedness of Heaven and the reality of the coming resurrection.

If the person who has died gave no evidence of being a Christian, the matter of his eternal destiny may come up. The child in a Christian home no doubt knows that only people who believe on Jesus go to Heaven. He may ask about a grandparent or uncle who apparently was not saved. Again, I believe it is a terrible mistake to lie to the child. We confuse a youngster when we give the impression that this person surely went to be with the Lord.

Telling the truth doesn't mean that we must come out and declare that the individual who died is suffering in a mass of flames. That's going beyond what we can truthfully say, for we don't know what may have transpired between that loved one and the Lord just before he died. Therefore, I believe we should express it to the child something like this: "I don't know whether Grandpa went to Heaven or not. He never said that he believed on Jesus, but we hope he did before he died. We just have to leave this up to God, and we are sure that He is going to do what is right for Grandpa." This is usually enough to satisfy the inquisitive child. He knows Hell is a place where he doesn't want to go, and that Heaven is to be greatly preferred.

In a time of death, don't forget the children! They need comfort too. They are able to face reality with amazing composure. And they can understand spiritual truth far better than we may be inclined to think.

Remember the Practical Needs

The final guideline for those who wish to exercise the Christian ministry of comfort is to remember the practical needs of the sorrowing. Right after the death, there may be a house to clean, children to care for, and meals to be prepared. When you see these needs, offer your services and then get busy. All too often the friends of the bereaved will say, "If there is anything I can do, just let me know." This is a useless statement! In the first place, the sorrowing people don't know for sure that you really mean what you're saying. Second, they don't know how much they can ask you to do. And third, they may not be aware of what will help them. Therefore, offer a specific service that you see is needed, and relieve them of the annoying little problems which aggravate their grief.

The bereaved one also needs companionship and friendship after the funeral, especially if he or she has lost a mate. From the time of the death until the funeral, the sorrowing are kept busy. The full impact of the loss may not come until later. A period of intense loneliness and deep grief which can last for months may cause the sorrowing person to think the wound is never going to heal. If he has been left alone, he will need companionship. This should come first from the sons and daughters. The Bible makes it clear that children are responsible to honor their parents, and this certainly includes spending time with them when they are aged or left alone. The other relatives and friends should also realize that taking this person out occasionally for a meal, a concert, or a church service will be greatly appreciated, and will help him adjust to his loss. If you're going to spend an evening with another couple, therefore, invite the widow or widower to join you. Then be natural and try to have a good time. You can be a good Christian friend just by being yourself.

You will make the bereaved person feel needed and wanted, and you will please the Lord.

The valley of grief can be long, dark, and lonely. Some desperately need help to get through it successfully. In Christian love and concern, you can offer that help. The Lord will give you insight and strength as you need it, and will enable you to extend godly sympathy and understanding. Pray for that person. See if you can find practical ways to help him cope with his grief and make his burden easier to bear. As you do, you will experience the joy of ministering effectively in the name of the Lord.

6

What Comes after Death?

What happens to us after we die? Are we simply unconscious until the resurrection? Or will we immediately join our friends and loved ones who have gone before? Will we stand before our Maker for judgment right after we die? Or will this event occur at the end of the world? If there is an intermediate state, what will it be like? What kind of bodies will we receive in the resurrection? Will life in Heaven be anything like it is on earth? These are a few of the many questions that come to people's minds when they are brought face to face with death.

The answers are to be found within the pages of the Bible. And, no one has the right to add to what the Scripture says, nor to be silent in areas where it gives us information. We are aware that the so-called "Christian" cults often distort what the Bible says about death. But sadly, many sincere believers also err when they go beyond the specific statements of God's Word. I attended a funeral recently and heard the minister portray the deceased, who had been an avid sportsman, as enjoying in Heaven the best hunting and fishing he had ever known. That preacher was using his imagination to say something nice, but he was certainly not declaring anything God has revealed.

I must admit that there are many mysteries about the life beyond. That doesn't trouble me, however, because there is also much I cannot comprehend about the world I live in now. About 40 years ago somebody told me the day would come when we would be able to watch a baseball game on a screen in our own home. I thought this was a pipe dream—almost too good to be true. I still don't understand how television works, but I no longer say it's impossible. Similarly, because I have already experienced the reality of God's presence and power, I'm not disturbed about the mysteries of eternity.

The person who has known the joy of salvation is content to trust God about the future. Just realizing that Heaven will be better than anything earth offers, and that he'll be with Jesus forever, is enough to satisfy his heart and mind. Besides, even though the Scriptures don't give many of the details about the hereafter, they do contain a number of vital truths about it for our instruction and comfort. In this chapter I will present a brief summary of the biblical concepts of the intermediate state, the resurrection, the judgment, and our eternal home.

The Intermediate State

What happens to a person right after he dies? In theology, this time is referred to as the "intermediate state," because it involves the period between death and resurrection. The Scriptures teach that the dead continue to be conscious, and that they are completely separated from the living—like being behind a wall no one can climb over or through.

A number of New Testament passages indicate that believers who have died are with Christ right now. While on the cross, Jesus told the repentant thief, "Verily I say unto thee, Today shalt thou be with Me in paradise" (Luke 23:43). Our Savior was asserting that He and the thief would meet that very day in paradise. Some cultists deny this truth, teaching rather that the soul goes completely out of existence between death and resurrection. They therefore punctuate this verse differently, to make our Lord say, "Verily I say unto thee today, shalt thou be with Me in paradise." But they can point to no other places in Scripture where Jesus said, "Verily I say unto thee today." Furthermore, using the word "today" in this way would be redundant, expressing the obvious. But our Lord used it for a definite purpose—to assure the suffering malefactor that his deliverance from pain and his entrance into paradise would occur that very day.

The epistles of Paul also teach that physical death ushers believers directly into the presence of Jesus Christ. In 2 Corinthians 5, the apostle said that he would rather live until Christ returns than go through the experience of dying. But he went on to declare that he wasn't afraid of death. Why? Because he was confident that the moment he would leave his body, he would be "present with the Lord" (see 2 Corinthians 5:6-9). He expressed the same assurance in Philippians 1:21-23, where he said that he had ambivalent feelings about dying. On the one hand, he saw it as "gain" and as being "with Christ, which is far better." But on the other hand, his love for his fellow-believers made him want to stay on earth and continue his ministry with them. Obviously, he did not conceive of the intermediate state as unconsciousness, for he spoke of it as "gain," and as being "with Christ."

The book of the Revelation contains two passages which indicate that between death and resurrection the soul of the believer is both conscious and happy. In Revelation 6:9-11, John tells us that the "souls of them that were slain for the word of God" were asking the Lord how long it would be before He would bring judgment upon the wicked and vindicate His cause. This is clearly a description of the state of believers between death and resurrection. The expression, "the souls of them that were slain," could only refer to the non-material aspect of the martyrs—that which survives death. Without question, they were conscious and were in the presence of the Lord.

The happiness of the redeemed between death and resurrection is further attested in Revelation 14:13, "Blessed are the dead who die in the Lord. . . . Yea, saith the Spirit, that they may rest from their labors, and their works do follow them." How wonderful is this picture of comfort and repose! Aged people have told me that extreme weariness often makes them long for rest. They say, "O how I long to be free from this terrible feeling of tiredness." That's why the biblical references to death as "sleep" are so beautiful. The weary body "sleeps" in the grave, while the soul enjoys perfect tranquillity in Heaven. The toilworn Christian can truly rejoice in the assurance that death will bring him sweet and welcome relief from the weariness of his earthly labor and sorrow.

In addition to being conscious and happy, the soul of the departed believer is completely out of touch with earth. We therefore cannot talk to those who have gone on, and they can't communicate with us. This truth needs emphasis in our day, because the spiritists and mediums who claim to be able to reach the dead are deceiving millions. Only God knows how much money is being spent in vain by people trying to communicate with loved ones who have gone on before. They are actually attempting something the Bible says cannot be done. The rich man, who had no regard for poor Lazarus during life, was in great distress after he died and wanted to send a message of warning to his brothers on earth. But his request was flatly refused. If people won't listen to God's servants on earth, they wouldn't respond any differently if someone returned from the realm of the dead to warn them.

Furthermore, to make an attempt to contact the dead is wicked, and is an act of disobedience to God. The prophet Isaiah strongly denounced all necromancy as sin. "And when they shall say unto you, Seek unto those who are mediums, and unto wizards that peep, and that mutter: should not a people seek unto their God? Should they seek on behalf of the living to the dead? To the law and to the testimony; if they speak not according to this word, it is because there is no light in them" (Isaiah 8:19, 20).

Don't ignore these biblical warnings! They can keep you from being manipulated by charlatans who are in the business for personal profit. Besides, you may become directly involved with the devil and his evil spirits. If supernatural activity does occur, it must be the work of demons or wicked angels who impersonate the dead. Anyone who practices spiritism places himself in danger of being in contact with the kingdom of evil, ruled over by Satan himself.

It's comforting to know that God has completely separated the dead from us. They therefore cannot see our sins, our cares, and our suffering. This isn't contradicted by Hebrews 12:1, which refers to the saints in glory as a "cloud of witnesses." The verse actually means that during their lifetime they had borne witness to the possibilities of the life of faith. The point the inspired writer is making is not that they see us, but that we should look to their example for encouragement and inspiration. It would mar the joy of the redeemed in Heaven if they had to observe the suffering, sin, and heartache of life on earth.

Then, too, believers who have been called Home are occupied with the things of Heaven, and are no longer concerned with the affairs of earth. I like to think, however, that God lets them know through the ministry of angels when one of their loved ones is saved. Remember, Jesus said that there is joy in the presence of the angels when a sinner is converted. The Lord may also inform them about significant happenings on earth which fit into His prophetic program. But the fact remains that the dead are separated from the living by a chasm which cannot be crossed.

In summary, all who have died in Christ are now at peace with Him in glory. Paul portrays their state as "gain" and as "far better" than life on earth. They are now resting from all their labors, for their souls are free from anxiety and their bodies are "asleep" in the grave. They are fully conscious and perfectly happy as they await the day of resurrection.

Resurrection

The intermediate state will continue until the time of Christ's second coming, when every believer will be resurrected from the grave. Paul described this event as follows: "Behold, I show you a mystery: We shall not all sleep, but we shall all be changed, in a moment, in the twinkling of an eye, at the last trump; for the trumpet shall sound, and the dead shall be raised incorruptible, and we shall be changed" (1 Corinthians 15:51, 52). We don't know exactly what the glorified bodies of the saints will look like, and we have no knowledge of their chemical composition. But we do have a number of comforting assurances about the resurrection body in the Bible.

First, it will be like the one Jesus Christ has today. In 1 John 3:2 we read, *"we shall be like Him; for we shall see Him as He is."* Paul tells us that we will be "fashioned like His glorious body" (Philippians 3:21). In 1 Corinthians 15 he declares that even as in this life we possess a body in the image of Adam, our earthly progenitor, so in Heaven we will have a body like that of the last Adam, the Lord Jesus Christ. This is a significant revelation, for we are told a number of things about our Lord's resurrection body. We know, for example, that it was real and tangible, for He showed His disciples His hands and His side, invited Thomas to touch His wounds, and allowed the women to clasp His feet in adoring worship. He ate food after His resurrection. But apparently He was free from the restrictions of our material world, for He could appear in a room where every window and door were closed.

We learn more about our resurrection bodies from 1 Corinthians 15:42-50. They will be immortal, in contrast to their present corruptibility. They will be glorious, not subject to the defilements that come through illness, aging, or an unclean environment. They will be powerful, no longer weak and subject to disease. Finally, they will be dominated by the spirit, suited to the environment of Heaven rather than being under the control of physical impulses and adapted for earthly living.

The Lord Jesus said that in our new bodies we will be like the angels of God, for "in the resurrection they neither marry, nor are given in marriage" (Matthew 22:30). This, of course, does not mean that we will be exactly like the angels, for 1 Corinthians 6:2, 3 tells us that we will be exalted above them. Instead, it means that our present physical similarity to the animal world in manner of conception, birth, and nourishment will cease, and that we will live on a far higher plane than was possible while we were citizens of earth.

As noted earlier, the Bible doesn't give us all the details we would like to know about our resurrection bodies. But it does reveal enough to enable us to look forward eagerly to the life beyond. We know that our personal identities will continue and that we will recognize one another. Our resurrection bodies will possess a grandeur far beyond anything we've ever seen on earth. In 1 Corinthians 15:35-38, Paul implies that our present physical structure can be compared to a tiny seed, while our glorified body can be likened to the luxuriantly beautiful flower that springs from the ground. It will be wonderful beyond description!

Judgment

Following the resurrection of the body, every Christian will stand before Jesus Christ to be judged. The apostle Paul declared, "For we must all appear before the judgment seat of Christ, that everyone may receive the things done in his body, according to that he hath done, whether it be good or bad" (2 Corinthians 5:10). This judgment will *not* be to determine our eternal destiny in either Heaven or Hell; that issue was settled the moment we received Jesus Christ as Savior. Rather, its purpose will be to bring up for review the spiritual caliber of our lives and the quality of our works.

We will be made to see the worthlessness of everything we did out of carnal, worldly, or selfish motives. We will be reminded of our unconfessed and unforsaken sins. Since Jesus Christ bore on Calvary all the punishment we deserved, we won't experience a further outpouring of God's wrath. But we undoubtedly will feel a sense of shame and will regret our halfhearted devotion, our self-centeredness, and our disobedience.

But this is only one side of the picture. We will also be given rewards for service motivated by love, for the Bible speaks of the bestowment of crowns. This doesn't mean we'll walk around Heaven with crowns on our heads, nor does it imply that believers will be separated into groups marked "super-spiritual," "somewhat spiritual," and "unspiritual." I see these rewards as the granting of different capacities for appreciation. Some will be given a greater potential for enjoying Heaven's beauties than others. It may be compared to the difference between a well-trained musician and someone like me who knows little about music listening to a concert. The virtuoso will appreciate the performance more than I, even though my pleasure is very real as far as it goes. This may not be a perfect illustration of how we will be rewarded in Heaven, but it offers a suggestion which has been helpful to me.

The judgment seat of Christ will be a solemn event, but the Lord does not want us to have a morbid dread of it. Remember, it will not entail punishment. Though we may be ashamed and humbled as we see our failures, we will be thrilled as we experience God's great forgiveness and amazing grace. We'll be in perfect agreement with the decisions of the Judge, for we will have a new comprehension of God's holiness, as well as of His love.

In the light of this coming judgment, let us become greatly concerned here and now about developing the fruit of the Spirit in our lives—"love, joy, peace, longsuffering, gentleness, goodness, faith, meekness, self-control" (Galatians 5:22, 23). If we are sound in doctrine and growing steadily to spiritual maturity, we will build upon the foundation of our faith in Christ a superstructure made of gold, silver, and precious stones—elements which will not be burned away when we stand before the Lord. On the other hand, if we are unconcerned about our beliefs and practices, we build a life of wood, hay, and stubble—materials which will be consumed in the testing fires of judgment. Let's seek God's help as we construct the edifice of our lives, so that what we produce will endure!

Eternity

After having received their glorified bodies and having appeared before the judgment seat of Christ, believers will enter their eternal state as citizens of Heaven. What a glorious place this new home will be! It is described in Revelation 21 and 22 as a beautiful city, the new Jerusalem, and as a lovely garden, the paradise of God. The city will have a jeweled foundation, a jasper wall, gates of pearl, and streets of gold—all shimmering with the radiance of glory. The streets of gold suggest that we will walk in unblemished holiness in the sunshine of God's presence. The colorful assortment of precious stones, each shining with its own particular beauty, suggests the harmonious variety of God's children in Heaven. We will not be an indistinguishable mass of humanity, all looking and acting alike, but a fellowship of distinct individuals united in the bond of love. The description of the paradise of God in Revelation 22 is but a faint preview of the marvelous beauties in nature that will mark our eternal residence—a place of sparkling streams and luxuriant, fruitful trees, all untainted by sin and unmarred by death.

Yes, Heaven will be beautiful. Just think of it! No sin! No death! Jesus will be there! The saints of all the ages, including all of our loved ones who knew the Savior, will be our eternal companions. We will see and know one another as never before, and the love of God will permeate every relationship. Here on earth we aren't always open and honest. There we will have spirit-to-spirit communion. Every aspect of our beings will be as clear and lovely as transparent gold. And through all the ages of eternity we will grow in beauty and wisdom as we serve the Lord, fellowship with one another, and explore the wonders of our exciting new Home. Mysteries? Yes, some things are still unknown. But what a thrilling prospect! The contemplation of our future glory brings heavenly light to the valley of death, for it carries our thoughts to the infinite bliss that lies beyond.

7

Living
and Dying Happily

When I was a boy I memorized a compendium of Christian doctrine which began with the question, "How many things are necessary for you to know in order that you may live and die happily?" The answer was, "Three: first, how great my sins and miseries are; second, how I may be delivered from my sins and miseries; and third, how I can express my gratitude to God for this deliverance."

As I look back, it seems that the words "to live and die happily" made as much of an impression upon me as the answer. This is because I knew many Christians who were very happy, some in spite of circumstances which were far from pleasant. My grandmother, accidentally blinded at the age of 72, lived with a spiritual joy that made her delightful to be around. She maintained a happy spirit until she died at 86, having borne her affliction with triumphant grace for 14 years. Another woman I knew had three mongoloid sons who needed infant care until they died in their twenties; but despite the burden and sorrow, she was a radiant Christian until her own Homegoing. People observed that she lived and died happily, and they wondered how she could do it.

I also saw many Christians who did not have this same joy. I remember hearing them speak of death as fearsome and terrifying. They said they hoped all would be well with them, but they couldn't be sure. Others, who had everything to be happy about, were miserable and complaining until they died. I still meet believers today who can't reconcile themselves to the fact that their beloved family circle will inevitably be broken by death. A lady whose parents are in their eighties and are showing signs of failing health told me recently that sometimes she can't get to sleep because she has such a fear of their dying. She knows they are believers and acknowledges that they will be with Christ, yet a feeling of dread haunts her whenever she thinks about their Homegoing. She realizes she shouldn't feel this way, but doesn't know how to overcome it.

In this final chapter of *Light in the Valley*, I would like to show you how you can face death without fear. I realize that the finest Christian may become disturbed by an impending death in his family, but he need not be overwhelmed or defeated.

Believers can and should manifest to the world a calm and assured attitude toward death. The Bible tells us that our faith in Christ frees us from a morbid fear of dying. The writer of Hebrews declares that Jesus Christ became a member of the human race and died on the cross, "that through death He might destroy him that had the power of death, that is, the devil, and deliver them who, through fear of death, were all their lifetime subject to bondage" (Hebrews 2:14, 15). Many peo-

ple have been weakened and enslaved by the fear
of death, but this should never be true of you as a
Christian. You should look upon death as a defeated foe, as a vanquished enemy who can never
really harm you. Yes, you can both live and die
happily, but you will not obtain this blessing auto-
matically. To do so, you must (1) make sure you
are saved, (2) keep in touch with the Lord, (3)
obey God's commandments, and (4) keep Heaven
in view. As you meet these four requirements, you
will become triumphant over the fear of death.

Make Sure You Are Saved

The first prerequisite to victory over the fear of
death is a genuine assurance of personal salvation.
You must be sure you're saved. It's one thing to
be able to give a glib testimony when your health
is good and everything is going well, but it's quite
another thing when you stand face to face with
death. I have known Christians who refused to
go to a funeral home to pay their respects to a
bereaved friend or relative. I have seen men and
women active in Christian service go to pieces
when a loved one died, or when they received
bad news about their own physical condition. It
seemed that they were just as much afraid of
death as people who did not believe in Christ.

I have deliberately used the word "Christian" to
describe people who are afraid of death, because
this fear may be present in the lives of true believers. But I must also recognize another possibility: some who profess faith in Christ are not
truly saved. One can give mental assent to biblical
teaching without accepting Jesus Christ as Savior.
The Lord declared that some of the people who
performed miracles in His name will be excluded
from Heaven because they never trusted in Him

for their salvation. Paul issued this solemn warning: "Examine yourselves, whether you are in the faith; prove yourselves" (2 Corinthians 13:5).

Were you sincere when you made your profession of believing on Jesus Christ, or did you just go through the motions to please someone? Did you believe that you were lost and that Jesus Christ died to pay the price for your sins? If you can say, "Yes, I meant what I said when I accepted Christ, and I believe everything the Bible says about Him," you can rest assured that you are indeed born again. What you need to do now is take God at His Word in the matter of death just as you did for your salvation. He has said that you are justified from all your sin, that you are a member of His family, that the power of death was broken through Christ's resurrection, and that you are destined to receive a resurrection body and spend eternity in Heaven. The Lord means what He says, and He is honored when you believe Him.

If after self-examination you aren't sure you have accepted Jesus Christ as your Savior, or if you realize that you only went through the motions, I urge you to make sure. Open your heart and receive Him right now. I remember that in my teens I had doubts about my salvation. I had asked Jesus Christ to come into my heart, and had said all the right things. But, like many young people, I had misgivings. They finally disappeared, however, when late one night I prayed something like this: "Dear Father, I'm not sure whether or not I've ever really accepted Jesus Christ as my Savior. I do believe that He died to pay the price for my sins. I believe what the Bible says about His resurrection. If I've never received Him before, I take Him right now." From that time on I felt a strong sense of reassurance, and was able to live confidently again.

As a pastor, I have dealt with scores of people who were just as uncertain as I was, and I've led them to do what I did. I have even suggested that they mark the date on their calendar as the time they arrived at certainty about their salvation. My friend, if you're not sure you are saved, settle the matter now. There is very little to be gained in fretful wondering about that earlier profession of faith. Make sure right now by doing what I did some 40 years ago. If you do, you will have fulfilled the first requirement for deliverance from the fear of death, for you will know you are a Christian.

Keep in Touch with God

A second means of attaining a deep spiritual peace which is not disturbed by the thought of death is to maintain fellowship with God. As a Christian, you need to feed on the Scriptures, to pray, to meditate, and to wait upon the Lord. When we are saved, the Lord gives us a new life. We have a new nature. That's what we mean when we speak about being "born again." But this new life needs to be fed and developed by reading the Bible and communing with God.

Many Christians have no spiritual depth because they are caught up in a ceaseless round of activity that leaves no time for private devotions. Then they wonder why they can't seem to gain victory over the sins that trouble them. They can't understand why they are so anxious and afraid when circumstances become unpleasant. The answer is not difficult to find; they never stop rushing around long enough to obey the Lord's exhortation, "Be still, and know that I am God" (Psalm 46:10). How important that we heed Peter's admonition, "As newborn babes, desire the pure milk of the word, that ye may grow by it" (1 Peter 2:2).

Yes, you may be busy, but you are not too busy to commune with God every day through Bible reading, meditation, and prayer. You will never be a steadfast, victorious believer without a regular devotional life.

Obey God's Commandments

The third requirement for deliverance from the fear of death is obedience to God's commandments. While salvation is a free gift, the fullness of joy and peace comes by doing the will of the Lord. Jesus promised, "If ye keep My commandments, ye shall abide in My love" (John 15:10). John declared, "And by this we do know that we know Him, if we keep His commandments" (1 John 2:3). Then, too, we receive the filling of the Holy Spirit through obedience. These familiar words are an express command: "And be not drunk with wine, in which is excess, but be filled with the Spirit" (Ephesians 5:18). The measure of our obedience to God's commands is the measure of our fullness of the Holy Spirit. Joyous expressions of praise in song and gratitude in prayer will be the natural outflow of your Spirit-filled life (see Ephesians 5:19, 20).

Dear saint of God, if you are apprehensive at the thought of dying, one of the reasons may be your disobedience to God. It's not a matter of your needing some new experience at all. I have known many Christians who had the idea that becoming a Spirit-filled believer is a very complicated and difficult process. They would attend revival meetings and go forward repeatedly to rededicate themselves to the Lord. They would go to Bible conference after Bible conference, hoping to gain some new understanding that would work like magic in their lives. But all they found was another temporary victory followed by another period of failure and defeat. They did not become stable and happy Christians until they realized that the Spirit-filled life comes when we sincerely set ourselves to obey the Lord.

When Jesus spoke of keeping His commandments, He didn't have in mind that His followers try to live up to the Decalogue of Exodus 20 or Deuteronomy 5. The Old Testament contains marvelous truths and wonderful principles for Christian living, but the specific commands to you and me are to be found in the New Testament. They appear on almost every page. We are given the charge to love our enemies, to pray for people who persecute us, to go the extra mile, to forgive others as God has forgiven us, to be kind, to be patient, to be faithful, and to be pure. We who are husbands are exhorted to love our wives. Wives are to be submissive to their husbands. Parents are to bring up their children in the nurture and admonition of the Lord, and to set a good example before them. Children are to obey and honor their parents. We are called upon to be faithful in church attendance. We are to give systematically, sacrificially, and cheerfully. And we are commanded to resist the devil, to put on the whole armor of God, to pray for all men, and to be obedient to civil authorities.

These are just a few of the commandments found in the New Testament. There are many more, and God expects you to take them all seriously. The old hymn is right when it says, "Trust and obey, for there's no other way to be happy in Jesus, but to trust and obey."

In closing this section, let me remind you of a marvelous promise Jesus gave His disciples. "He that hath My commandments, and keepeth them, he it is that loveth Me; and he that loveth Me shall be loved of My Father, and I will love him, and will manifest Myself to him" (John 14:21). Yes, obedience to Christ brings freedom from fear, doubt, and anxiety. And it helps prepare the believer for the valley of death.

Keep Heaven in View

The fourth requirement for a serene attitude toward death is to cultivate an awareness of eternity, which puts the things of time in proper perspective. The apostle Paul urged believers to do this when he wrote, "If ye, then, be risen with Christ, seek those things which are above, where Christ sitteth on the right hand of God. Set your affection on things above, not on things on the earth" (Colossians 3:1, 2).

In this materialistic age we easily become so enmeshed in the activities and pleasures of this world that we give little thought to Heaven. I have called on believers in failing health who were far more interested in talking about the news, sporting events, or the stock market than about the things of the Lord. I repeatedly directed the conversation back to the spiritual for the person's own good. Although believing on Christ, people like this are actually avoiding a confrontation with reality. They are loath to admit that they will die. They may confess their faith in Christ and His resurrection, but in practice they suppress all somber thoughts of death and dying, or sublimate them by becoming absorbed in their work, an avocation, or entertainment. As a result, they never progress to a spiritually mature view of Heaven and eternity, and do not die happily.

How can we develop a perspective that will enable us to set our affection on things above? I have already pointed out the necessity of maintaining a personal devotional life and of obeying the commands of the Bible. Let me offer two further suggestions: (1) We should remind ourselves of human frailty and the temporary nature of this life. (2) We should openly discuss death and the hereafter with people we know and love.

We would do well to read the Psalms as a reminder that our earthly existence is transitory. In Psalm 49, for example, God's children are warned that people who live only for this world will die "like the beasts that perish." To the psalmist this was a tragedy, for man is more than an animal.

In Psalm 39 we read this beautiful prayer expressing the desires of one who is acutely aware of the brevity of life: "Lord, make me to know mine end, and the measure of my days, what it is, that I may know how frail I am. Behold, Thou hast made my days as an handbreadth, and mine age is as nothing before Thee. Verily every man at his best state is altogether vanity. Selah. Surely every man walketh in a vain show; surely they are disquieted in vain; he heapeth up riches, and knoweth not who shall gather them. And now, Lord, what wait I for? My hope is in Thee" (Psalm 39:4-7).

When we turn to Psalm 90, a literary masterpiece, we see the shortness of man's span on earth contrasted with God's eternity. We can pray with Moses in response, "So teach us to number our days, that we may apply our hearts unto wisdom" (Psalm 90:12). In the New Testament, James asks, "For what is your life? It is even a vapor that ap-

peareth for a little time, and then vanisheth away"
(James 4:14).

The reality of death ought to be a constant part
of our thinking, for when we view life in the
perspective of eternity, we will evaluate it prop-
erly. We won't set our affection on things of the
earth. I recall a statement made by an elderly
Christian as he viewed the beautiful home that
one of his friends in his early seventies had just
built. He said something like this: "Brother, this
is a lovely house, but don't place too much value
on it. Remember, you'll soon be leaving it. Don't
let your roots go down too deep in this old world,
because one of these days you're going to be up-
rooted; and the deeper they go, the more it's going to hurt." The Bible tells us again and again
that we are sojourners here. Your earthly life and
mine is a pilgrimage. Everything material will one
day perish. But spiritual realities are eternal, and
the joys related to them will last forever. When
this truth is reflected in your lifestyle, you will be
able to live and die happily.

Another help in developing a gradual detach-
ment from earth and a growing desire for Heaven
is honest and open discussion of death and the
hereafter with the people we love. In the midst
of life's best days, husbands and wives should plan
for the time when one of the partners is taken.
The funeral, the financial picture, and the other
practical matters should be carefully considered.
After all, as Christians we are convinced that it's
the survivor, not the one who has gone to Heaven,
who needs help and guidance. It's not morbid to
talk about death when the discussion is carried on
in the light of what the Bible says. Rather, it is
healthy, for it brings the subject out in the open
where it can be seen for what it really is. Death

is not the king of terrors, it's the doorway to Glory.

As I conclude this book, I remind you once again of the hopelessness of life apart from Jesus Christ. People who have never trusted in Him may be able to steel themselves to meet the grim reaper with raw courage. They may even conjure up a glimmer of hope by entertaining the thought that maybe something good lies beyond this world. But that's all they can do.

If you are not saved, I urge you to take an honest look at yourself. Then consider the claims of Jesus Christ. The Christian faith is reasonable, grounded in history, and confirmed in the experience of millions. Even intellectual giants have testified both to the credibility of the New Testament message and to its transforming power.

When you accept what the Bible says about Christ's birth, life, miracles, death, and resurrection, and when you acknowledge your need for Divine forgiveness and believe in the Lord Jesus, you will discover the beauty of life and the meaning of death. You will be able to rise each morning with a prayer of gratitude for the privilege of entering a new day. The world will be filled with beauty, and you will see people differently than you ever did before. Death, that phenomenon which was once so frightening, will have lost its terror. You will even contemplate your own passing without fear. And when a Christian loved one dies, you will be comforted, and have an added reason for looking forward to the glorious day of reunion on the other shore.

Take Jesus Christ as your Savior today. He'll enable you to live and die happily. He'll illuminate your path, and when the valley of the shadow of death lies before you, He'll flood it with light.

8

What About Mercy Killing?

I recently went to a nursing home to visit a friend. Passing a doorway, I heard cries that sounded like a wounded animal. I couldn't help but look in. What I saw made my heart sink. An aged person (whether man or woman I don't know), on hands and knees in a bed with protective railings, was making eerie, pathetic, almost inhuman sounds. My thoughts went up to God in silent appeal. "Lord, why do you let a human being, created in Your image, become like this? How can You be glorified through one who has lost almost every semblance of humanity?"

Those who believe in euthanasia, the technical name for mercy killing, say they have the answer to the problem of prolonged human agony. They insist, "It would be an act of mercy for the doctor to administer a simple injection and quietly end the suffering one's life. It would be much better for the patient and certainly easier for the relatives. We don't even let a helpless or deranged animal continue to live—why not be as kind to humans?"

These arguments at first may sound quite convincing. But if we are well-versed in the Scriptures, we will not accept them. The Bible teaches that God made man in His own image and likeness and that human life is far different from that of an animal. If we are parents, we experienced a deep sense of wonder when our baby was born. The marvel of its own individuality and development brought us feelings of awe and wonder. Somehow we can't escape the conviction that when a child is taken by death, grief-stricken parents who believe in God still find that the words of Job, when he received the news that his children had been killed, express their own emotions: "The Lord gave, and the Lord hath taken away; blessed be the name of the Lord" (Job 1:21). Deep within, we have the conviction that since God alone can give life, He alone has the right to take it.

An advocate of mercy killing views human life as essentially the same as animal life. He easily concludes that it's best to spare from needless suffering all who have no hope of recovery. In fact, one writer has suggested that when the world becomes heavily overpopulated, everybody beyond a certain age (he suggests 60) should go voluntarily to a place where, surrounded by beautiful flowers and lovely music, he accepts a painless but lethal drug that will put him to sleep forever. A number of problems about the treatment of people who are dying must be faced. Tremendous advances in medical technology have taken us beyond the simple choices of the past. At one time the only alternative for an incurable illness was to let the person live until he died. In those days almost everybody said, "Hands off. We must leave the time of his death with God." But now, doctors and sometimes loved ones are called upon to make a decision between letting a person die, or keeping him alive by the use of life-support machines.

These developments have raised perplexing new questions: Is it all right for a doctor who is convinced that the end of life is imminent and unavoidable to shut off or disconnect a machine so that death may come quickly? If I go to the hospital with an illness doctors say is terminal, do I have a right to request them not to use these new machines to keep me alive for a few additional weeks or months of semiconscious or unconscious existence? Is it permissible for the family of a loved one in a coma who has suffered irreversible brain damage to demand that life-supporting measures be discontinued?

Certain Christian principles may answer questions like this. A settlement of this issue would also offer help in the emotional struggle people go through when loved ones continue to live on though suffering and totally irrational.

What Man Is

Regardless of physical or mental condition, people are more than mere organisms that go out of existence when their last breath is taken. The unique moral and spiritual element in man is what lies behind the divine prohibitions of adultery, fornication, murder, theft, and deceit. If we were not rational and moral creatures, these rules would be both meaningless and pointless. But because we are made in God's image, we have rights, privileges, duties, and responsibilities that mere animals do not have.

Occasions do arise when the doctors decide to prescribe a pain-relieving medicine for a patient even though they know this drug may hasten the onset of death. The purpose for administering the medication determines whether it is right or wrong. It would be wrong to refuse to give the medication and let the patient go through several days or weeks of unnecessary and pointless torture.

Allowing Death Is Sometimes Right

Christians need to be sympathetic to the difficult choices a doctor treating terminally ill patients is often forced to make. He must decide whether or not to use heroic measures to sustain the physical functions of a person who is no longer capable of knowing who or where he is. The physician may see this brief extension of life as only adding to the suffering of both the patient and his loved ones; yet he has taken a pledge to maintain life as long as possible. He is also painfully aware of the possibility of a malpractice suit if a relative decides to claim negligence. He often hesitates to discuss alternatives with the patient's relatives knowing it only adds to their stress. Later they might have terrible feelings of guilt for participating in a decision that brought a quick death to their loved one.

When the conscientious physician has difficult decisions to make about the propriety of using respirators, heart stimulators, or other life-supporting equipment, he has a number of considerations in mind. If someone very close to me were in the final stages of illness, and every day only extended the extreme torture, I would pray for the Lord to take him or her quickly. Then, if the doctor told me that disconnecting a machine would abbreviate the time of suffering, I would gratefully give my consent.

In his book, *The View from a Hearse*, Joseph Bayly tells about one of his friends who deliberately hastened his own death. In the hospital pitifully weak and dying, he had been told that he could not live longer than a week or two. One Sunday night, after a beautiful visit with his wife, he pulled the needle which was sustaining his life from his arm, turned off the valve, and went to sleep. He died the next day. I agree with Dr. Bayly's assertion that this man did not commit suicide. All he did was remove an instrument which was doing nothing but prolonging his own pain, extending his wife's grief, and postponing his entrance into Glory.

When a Christian goes to the hospital with a terminal illness, I believe he has a right to ask the doctors not to prolong his life needlessly and pointlessly. We who believe in Christ have the confidence that "to die is gain" (Phil. 1:21). We would far rather be in Heaven than lying half-conscious on a bed of pain. We would rather have our loved ones on that other shore than here in a pitiable state. While we shouldn't deliberately end life, we can let death come by discontinuing life-supporting procedures that at best only delay the inevitable by a few days or weeks. To keep alive someone with extensive damage to vital organs by means of a breathing machine or by intravenous flow of medicine and nourishment is cruel.

The Exercise of Faith Gives Victory

A believer who exercises faith can have victory in all of life's circumstances—even those we have described. Hard as it is to suffer intense pain, many of God's children have been marvelously triumphant. Their testimonies have tremendous impact upon others. Their loved ones have been strengthened and edified by observing the victorious outlook of those who are striking demonstrations of God's grace.

The suffering person isn't always able to give a glowing witness, however, which makes it more difficult for those who stand by. Some unsaved people who observe such a deathbed scene become bitter and use the incident as an excuse for rejecting God and His salvation. I have also known believers who became angry and resentful under similar circumstances.

The strain is even more difficult when a loved one becomes senile or loses his mental faculties. Loved ones become disturbed when the person they once knew changes so drastically. But even then spiritual victory is possible through prayer and God's Word. An attitude of submission will help them experience God's marvelous grace. I'll admit that it isn't easy to understand how the Lord will bring good out of the hopeless senility or irrationality of one of His children. But we can enjoy peace of heart and mind if we heed God's Word. Three of its truths are helpful in such times of distress.

Trust God in the Dark

Christians must trust God even when they don't understand His way. Trust becomes easier when we reflect upon our smallness as compared to His greatness. Job and his three friends thought through the situation carefully trying to find the reason for his affliction, but they never really arrived at an answer. It was only when the Lord spoke to him directly, telling him to reflect upon the great difference between the Almighty and a mere human being, that Job finally realized his insignificance and the folly of questioning God's ways. When you meet God through the pages of His Word and in prayer, you also will be able to trust the Almighty even when you don't understand His ways.

Don't Expect a Trouble-free Life

Second, meditate on the fact that the Bible does not guarantee believers exemption from suffering and distress which are in the world because of sin.

We are subject to the same illnesses and accidents others are. The arteries in the body of a believer harden just like they do in the worst sinner. When you accept this truth, you will no longer struggle with your faith about why Christians suffer. If, for example, you see a believer in a state of mental derangement as a result of a cranial tumor or head injury, you'll be better able to accept it. If God were to make sure that no Christian would ever become senile or mentally deranged, we would have clinical proof for the validity of our Christian claims—but then we would no longer need to exercise faith.

The Lord both *reveals* and *conceals* Himself, so that people might make a spiritual or moral decision for salvation, rather than purely rational. He could easily give such unmistakable signs of His presence in the world that nobody would dare deny His existence. But if He did, men would no longer be called upon to make a moral or spiritual choice. Therefore, the Lord doesn't treat Christians as cosmic pets. He doesn't exclude us from the pain and suffering that is part and parcel of life on this planet.

Trust Brings Peace

Third, we can enjoy the inner certainty and peace the Holy Spirit produces in God's children who trust Him. Paul speaks of this ministry as "the Spirit witnessing with our spirit." The apostle himself experienced the Spirit's witness, and he wrote that *nothing* can separate us from the love of Christ (see Rom. 8:35-39).

A dedicated Christian *can* be victorious even when we see one we love become irrational, or waste away until he is a mere shadow of his former self. When we ourselves are called upon to go through great physical distress, we can be "more than conquerors." Through prayer, God's Word, and an attitude of submission, we can live and die happily.

When you witness suffering for which you can see no good reason, remind yourself of how little you know compared to God's omniscience. Recognize that God has called upon you to live by faith, and that you therefore cannot expect exemption from any of the temporal results of sin. Finally, submit to the Lord, so that you can experience the inner witness of the Holy Spirit. Then you will have that peace which Paul said "passeth all understanding."

I don't know what lies ahead for me on earth. I don't know if the Lord is going to call me Home by the rapture or through death. If I must die, I hope I won't have to suffer long, become helpless, or lose my mental faculties. Yet I cannot assume that none of these things will happen to me, or to someone I love. But of this I am certain: Nothing in all the world will be able to separate me from the love of God, which is in Christ Jesus, my Lord. What a tremendous guarantee! It's all I need! And it's yours too, if you believe in Christ as your Saviour.

9

The
Physical Remains

I remember my first encounter with funerals at five years old when an old friend of my parents passed away. I did not see his remains because his body was not embalmed. I don't remember much of the funeral service, but I vividly recall seeing the casket being lowered into the grave. Somehow I was troubled at the thought of this person being put in the dark ground. Later, my father told me what the Bible taught about death, assuring me that the man's soul was in heaven, and that his body was no more than an empty eggshell after the chick has left it. His explanation was very comforting to me.

This incident illustrates the importance of knowing what the Bible says about the body. Children should know about death as soon as they wonder about it. After my father explained what the Bible taught, I never again looked at a body in a casket without realizing that the person himself was no longer there. The Christian belief about death gives us emotional stability and sure direction when we must make decisions about the corpse of a loved one.

During my pastoral experience, I found that well-instructed Christians generally handle death well. They don't display the emotional excesses as others. Believers in Christ, even though they may weep in sorrow, can reflect upon the glory of the soul in Heaven, rather than brooding about what happens to the body.

I have seen distraught men and women speak to the corpse as if it could hear. I have watched close relatives of the decreased hurl themselves on the casket at the committal. But a believer who knows what the Bible teaches about death and appropriates it to himself in faith, can be composed, even at the cemetery. His tears will be from sorrow, not from bitterness or hopeless despair, because an irrational and excessively emotional attachment to the body of a loved one is actually a practical denial of the Christian faith.

Other bereaved ones have gone to the other extreme of flippant disrespect for the dead. They perhaps don't take this attitude toward the body of someone they love, but jokes or irreverent terms about corpses are offensive to me even though I know such talk is usually a cover-up for feelings of fear of death.

I am fully aware that bodies are useful in medical schools. But I believe that even then the cadaver, which was once the home of a soul, should be handled respectfully. For the Christian, the body is the temple of the Holy Spirit, and the vehicle of all we do and say. Though a lifeless form isn't pleasant to see, it is described by Paul as the "seed" from which a glorified body will someday emerge. God places value upon it, and so should we.

Should I Allow an Autopsy?

Often one of the first decisions to make when a loved one dies is whether or not to grant permission for a postmortem examination. Doctors may want to determine the exact cause of death, and the knowledge they gain through the autopsy may enable them to become more effective in treating people with similar conditions. I know of instances when the surviving spouse or children refused point-blank to allow a postmortem because they didn't like the thought of it.

The possibility that doctors may gain the knowledge to save another person's life is reason enough for me to believe such a decision is right. A mature Christian shouldn't conjure up a mental picture of what happens to the body during this procedure, since the soul is no longer in the empty shell that remains but is with Christ in Heaven. The doctor's work is not desecrating the body since nothing he does will affect the resurrected body.

What about Organ Transplants?

A second question is the matter of organ transplants. In our generation, hearts have been taken from people at death and successfully implanted in others with defective hearts. Some recipients had many years extended to their lives. The other day I drove behind a car with a bumper sticker reading, "Donate your kidneys. Don't bury them." Many people are grateful to be living normally today with kidneys received from the body of another. A good number of men and women are able to see today because of corneal transplants received from someone who stipulated before his death that his eyes be used for this purpose.

I occasionally meet people with reservations about organ transplants. Some of their uncertainty may be the result of ignorance. One lady said, "When I was saved, God gave me a new heart. If Jesus lives in it, it wouldn't be proper to give it to someone who isn't a Christian." Of course, she was confusing the biblical term "heart," which refers to the inner being of a person, with the organ that pumps blood through the body. Some people wonder if man has the right to treat organs of the body like parts of a machine. Because they believe in the resurrection they say we should leave the body of a deceased person intact.

I believe the removal of corneas or the taking of the kidneys does not in any sense show disrespect for a dead body. The doctrine of bodily resurrection gives no reason to refuse transplants. In the resurrection, believers in Jesus Christ will all receive perfect bodies, no matter what has happened to them on earth.

There is no biblical reason to say that doctors who transplant organs are stepping into forbidden territory. God has allowed men and women in scientific research to discover and develop amazing medical techniques. He built into the human body the possibility that, after proper cross-matching, it can function with a kidney taken from a person who has died. The scientists have only discovered how to make these laws of nature help us. God is still totally in control.

Does the Bible Prohibit Cremation?
The number of people making arrangements to have their bodies burned is growing, though they still represent only a small minority. Advocates say that it is cheaper, that it doesn't take up valuable land as cemeteries do, and less repugnant than the thought of slow deterioration which occurs with burial.

I cannot find any solid evidence in the Bible that

cremation is wrong. In fact, if some horrible disease were to strike a community, burning would be the safest and best way to dispose of the contaminated bodies. In general, however, I advise burial for the following reasons:

First, burial was practiced by both Hebrews and Christians. It was the custom of Hebrew people to put their dead in tombs. The Old Testament indicates that when a corpse was burned, it was usually an expression of contempt for that individual or his principles. Biblical and church history therefore tends to favor burial as the proper way to take care of a dead body.

Second, cremation was associated with the heathen during past ages. In more recent times, atheists requested it as an expression of their disbelief in the resurrection.

Third, in 1 Corinthians 15, Paul compares the resurrection body with a green and vigorous plant that comes from a seed placed in the ground. He speaks of our perishable, humiliating, weak, and earth-bound body as being "sown" into the earth. It is the "seed" from which will spring one that will be imperishable, glorious, powerful, and designed for heaven, a picture which suggests burial rather than cremation.

So cremation is not necessarily wrong, but seems less desirable than burial. Undoubtedly, many people who request it have no thought of acting in defiance against the Lord. Nor will cremation present a problem to God when He resurrects the bodies of the dead. But because Old Testament Jews, early Christians, and Jesus Himself were buried, and because burial corresponds beautifully with the picture of resurrection in 1 Corinthians 15, many prefer it to cremation.

What about the Traditional Funeral?

The traditional funeral involves a mortician and other expenses. The total cost—the funeral director's fee, the vault, the cemetery plot, and the charges for opening and closing the grave requires a sizable sum. Many widows, especially those with dependent children, could put this money to far better advantage.

The alternative usually offered is to bury the dead as soon as possible—either on the day of death or the next. A wooden box would be adequate protection for the remains. The Christians who advocate this procedure say a memorial service can replace a funeral.

This departure from custom is not unbiblical or wrong. Of course, local laws must be strictly obeyed. Sanitary precautions must be observed and other ordinances carefully followed. The owner of the land should find out whether or not he will be able to sell his property without designating the site of the burials.

If a family decides to follow this plan, I would not refuse to be the attending minister. Before relatives depart from the cultural norm, they should consider that certain disturbing thoughts will come to mind. What will people think? Will it look as if I don't care enough for my loved ones to spend the money for a funeral? Make sure you will be able to face these questions without feelings of guilt. Be sure to look into the legal requirements. Make all the plans *before* a member of the family dies. A day or two may not be enough to complete the necessary arrangements and to comply with the law.

I usually advise people to follow the customary funeral procedure. Relatives and friends coming to view the body and express their sympathy has great value. At the moment of death, the loved ones often feel a sense of numbness. Members of the immediate family can hardly believe death has really come. The hours spent standing near the casket, receiving the condolences of friends and relatives, enable the loved ones to accept the reality of the event to make the necessary emotional adjustments. After the funeral is over and the body is in its resting place, the family is then better able to face the fact of the empty chair.

Though the cost of a traditional funeral is a major consideration, people of moderate means need not select an expensive casket. Most funeral directors are very considerate and understanding with people who do not have much money to spend. Even when the only fee comes from public funds, and there is little or no profit, morticians generally treat the loved ones with kindness and courtesy. Their service is extremely helpful. They come to the home as soon as they can. They know just what to do, and this takes a great deal of strain off the family. They offer many helpful suggestions. Therefore, I would suggest that the traditional funeral procedure be carefully considered.

A Personal Word

Four principles have guided me in my ministry to bereaved families and in conducting funeral services:

1. *Read the Word of God and proclaim it with authority.*

   Beautiful sentiments and gushy poetry mean little to the grieving. The great biblical themes of sin and death, salvation and resurrection, give positive comfort and strength to the loved ones.

2. *Show compassion.*

   The grieving must be given the assurance that their sorrow is not displeasing to the Lord.

Avoid expressions of sentiment that might stimulate uncontrolled outbursts of emotion. The saved must be challenged to be "steadfast, immovable, always abounding in the work of the Lord," and the unsaved confronted with the fact of their lost condition. But the time of death is not the time to browbeat sorrowing people into submission to Christ.

3. *Help the bereaved to use good judgment.*
   The family may think that the most expensive funeral is the best way to show love to the one who has left, which straps themselves financially and causes regret later.

4. *Help the family face the future.*
   Sometimes a young widow with children or an older person needs assistance in unscrambling the maze of business and financial matters. Veterans' benefits, insurance payments, social security claims, and pension provisions are among the confusing array of practical realities with which the survivors may need help. A person who is knowledgeable in this area would perform a real service by offering his help.

Death is never an easy matter. The sense of sorrow and loss can be overwhelming. The grieving may feel totally unable to make the right decisions and take care of the practical matters. Yet a thorough understanding of God's Word, preparation beforehand, and a life of faith can make the time of grief easier and more glorifying to God.